TWO FAMILIES IN COLONIAL CHILE

TWO FAMILIES IN COLONIAL CHILE

Della M. Flusche

Latin American Studies
Volume 2

The Edwin Mellen Press
Lewiston/Lampeter/Queenston

HN
300
.Z9
E44
1989

Library of Congress Cataloging-in-Publication Data

Flusche, Della M.
   Two families in colonial Chile / Della M. Flusche.
     p.   cm. -- (Latin American studies ; v. 2)
   Bibliography: p.
   Includes index.
   ISBN 0-88946-491-X
   1. Elite (Social sciences)--Chile--History--17th century--Case studies.   2. Social mobility--Chile--History--Case studies.
3. Elite (Social sciences)--Chile--History--16th century--Case studies.   4. Irarrázaval family.   5. Toro Mazote family.
6. Santiago (Chile)--Biography.   7. Chile--Biography.   I. Title.
II. Series : Latin American studies   (Lewiston, N.Y.) ; v. 2.
HN300.Z9E44   1989
305.5'2'0983--dc19   88-39147
                                                                      CIP

> This is volume 2 in the continuing series
> Latin American Studies
> Volume 2 ISBN 0-88946-491-X
> LAS Series ISBN 0-88946-488-X

A CIP catalog record for this book
is available from the British Library.

© Copyright 1989 The Edwin Mellen Press.

All Rights Reserved. For more information contact

      The Edwin Mellen Press   The Edwin Mellen Press
              Box 450   Box 67
           Lewiston, NY   Queenston, Ontario
           USA 14092   CANADA L0S 1L0

The Edwin Mellen Press, Ltd.
Lampeter, Dyfed, Wales,
UNITED KINGDOM SA48 7DY

Printed in the United States of America

In Memory of

José Toribio Medina

CONTENTS

PREFACE	vii
INTRODUCTION	xi
PART I: Patricians	1
Chapter 1. The Young Cavalier	9
Chapter 2. In Quest of Rewards	35
Chapter 3. Settling in Chile	57
PART II: Social Climbers	87
Chapter 4. Obscure Family Origins	95
Chapter 5. Moving Up	103
Chapter 6. A Wealthy Notary	117
EPILOGUE	159
APPENDICES	
1. Abstracts of Church Records in Santiago, 1583-1682	173
2. Royal Revenue Derived from Toro Mazote Proprietary Offices, 1584-1674	
3. Abstracts of Notarial Records, 1622-1623	179
ABBREVIATIONS	195
NOTES	196
BIBLIOGRAPHY	223
INDEX	237

TWO FAMILIES IN COLONIAL CHILE

PREFACE

This small monograph examines the personal lives, individual aspirations, private enterprises, and public careers of colonists drawn from two representative families in Santiago, Chile. The rise of a merchant-professional-landowning clan to prominence in the seventeenth century is viewed in juxtaposition to a sixteenth-century family's undisputed claim to membership in the conquistador, patrician elite.

As explained more fully in the Introduction, Latin Americanists recognize that colonial society underwent considerable change. The task at hand is therefore to demonstrate the degree and process of change that occurred in specific circumstances and environments. The present study accordingly investigates how, when, and why certain changes took place in Chile during the Hapsburg era. The significance of upward social mobility can then be indicated more accurately. Similarly, the composition of the several upper strata will be better understood.

Not only the changing physical membership of social classes but also the constants or stabilizing factors in colonial society deserve analysis. One of these is the pervasive, enduring patrician ethos. Seeking a higher station in life implied an acceptance of aristocratic values.

In studying the characteristics of the sixteenth-century aristocracy in Part I, the patrician mentality is therefore included. This raises a series of questions. What self-image did patricians have? Where did it originate? How did it manifest itself? What sources are available to discover and study patrician values? What do the sources reveal about setting and reaching aristocratic goals? What mundane activities provided the means to effect an aristocratic lifestyle? Data regarding don Francisco de Irarrázaval y Andía, his wife doña Lorenza de Zárate, and their descendants provide partial answers to these queries.

While the structure of society remained rather static during the Hapsburg era, commoners altered the membership of the several strata as they found ways to advance themselves. These are sketched in the introduction to Part II. Since the Toro Mazote family is a prime example of upward social mobility, chapters 4, 5, and 6 trace the step-by-step process that these social climbers used to gain not only wealth but also stature. In the available sources, attitudes are important but subordinated to actions. The Toro Mazotes said less about themselves than did the proud Irarrázavals. The nature of the evidence therefore mandates a slight shift in emphasis. Bureaucratic, professional, and economic pursuits are accordingly studied in conjunction with marital, kinship, and friendly alliances.

A brief epilogue compares and contrasts the status of latter-day Irarrázavals and Toro Mazotes. To round out the contents, the analysis extends into the Bourbon century.

Three appendices complement the text. Appendix 1 compiles documentary abstracts drawn from parish records in Santiago that pertain to members of the two families. Appendix 2 consists of a table showing royal revenue derived from Toro Mazote proprietary offices. Appendix 3 summarizes notarial documents recorded in the office of Manuel de Toro Mazote.

I am indebted to many individuals and institutions for their help in the creation of this book. Eugene H. Korth, S.J., who first introduced me to the rich field of Chilean history and historiography, received a special thank you before his untimely death. He offered encouragement and generously lent his scholarly expertise to a critical evaluation of more than one draft of the manuscript. I am grateful to Eastern Michigan University for a Keal Award and a Faculty Research Fellowship. The latter enabled me to consult microfilmed materials in the Genealogical Society of Utah Library where the staff proved most helpful. I am also grateful to Nancy Snyder, Jill Bauer, Tammy Mull, and Martha Rogers who worked diligently to prepare a camera-ready copy of the text.

INTRODUCTION

The search for a better understanding of the colonial background of modern Latin American nations is producing a wealth of information on the nature and significance of social phenomena. The new data more clearly define the social structure that set the upper classes or elites above and apart from mere commoners who were themselves divided into middle and lower groups.

In reviewing recent literature and indicating directions for further research on socioeconomic questions in the Spanish American realms, Magnus Mörner discusses the related topics of structure and stratification. He perceives a general pattern of "a light-skinned elite superimposed on a mostly darker skinned conglomerate of strata." Mörner is concerned that better answers be forthcoming on the identity of individuals and groups that comprised a given stratum and acknowledges Mario Góngora's contributions to this subject.[1]

Góngora himself has gone far to name members of the upper strata in colonial Chile and to explain criteria for aristocratic standing. He modestly affirms, however, that his research stops short of an exhaustive analysis of genealogical sources.[2] These materials, as Mörner notes and as Jacques A. Barbier comments in regard to eighteenth-century elites, expand our knowledge of prominent colonials.[3]

While a relatively small number of specialists is familiar with the scholarly endeavors of Mörner, Góngora, and Barbier, a wider public has access to Brian Loveman's Chile: The Legacy of Hispanic Capitalism. This excellent general history is understandably concerned with the long range effects of the stratified structure of colonial society and takes little notice of the individual and familial components of the classes. Loveman accordingly does not elaborate on quarrels within families and factional disputes that divided the aristocracy against itself. Instead, he makes the following case for perceiving a homogeneous quality in the upper strata:

> An impressive ability to co-opt royal officials through business or marital ties and to absorb new wealth and successful immigrants created an integrated political, economic, and social elite with interests in agriculture, commerce, and mining. Intermarriage, shared social values, and dependence for economic well-being upon the exploitation of the rural labor force

unified the Chilean upper classes and helped forge a unique variant of Hispanic capitalism on the periphery of the Spanish Empire.[4]

This interpretation, based as it is on Loveman's thorough acquaintance with recent scholarship, has much validity. The elite did manifest these characteristics and, when viewed from without, appears unified.

The aristocracy closed ranks against threats to prerogative or privilege and cooperated to win concessions from the crown that would increase the local magnates' power, prestige, and profit. This was especially true, as Eugene H. Korth demonstrates, in regard to enslaving Araucanian prisoners of war and prolonging the Indian labor tribute known as "personal service."[5]

Korth and I have called attention to the inequities that the hierarchical socioeconomic structure perpetrated against women of African and Indian descent. We subsequently analyzed data concerning the feminine aspects of the predominantly white upper levels of society in colonial Chile. The findings we have presented on nonwhite women and our research on Hispanic females point to a diversity of individual experiences within a cohesive class structure.[6]

This present book seeks to clarify the internal characteristics of a small segment of society during the Hapsburg era. With biographical sketches that incorporate genealogical data, it represents a modest response to Magnus Mörner's call for more "life stories that will show the possible range of individual achievement and make colonial society a living reality."[7] A comprehensive response to his broad mandate is obviously beyond the scope of this limited endeavor. For those whose reading is confined to works in English, it stands chronologically between monographs by James Lockhart and Jacques A. Barbier. The former notes that a large group of dons arrived in Peru in the 1550s, and a number of them went on to Chile. The latter examines the eighteenth-century Chilean aristocracy that included the Irarrázaval and Toro Mazote families.[8] If this present brief volume fills in some of the gaps regarding men and women from these families who lived in the Long Land in the sixteenth and seventeenth centuries, it will have fulfilled its purpose. Questions that it cannot answer regarding them are respectfully deferred to Chilean historians.

PART I

PATRICIANS

The concepts and norms that differentiated the upper classes from the lower orders in Spanish American society originated in medieval Spain. When Columbus crossed the Atlantic under the auspices of Isabel of Castile, Renaissance values were modifying the older ideals that characterized Iberia in the Middle Ages. The effect of this historical process on Spanish America would be immediate and emphatic. The attitudes and patterns of behavior of the <u>conquistadores</u> and early colonists are a case in point.

Obvious examples can be drawn from the letters of Cortés to the Emperor Charles V, the chronicle of the conquest of New Spain by Bernal Díaz del Castillo and, more relevant to the present analysis, reports to the crown on Chilean conditions from the conquistador Pedro de Valdivia. A deep adherence to the Catholic faith, if not full compliance with its moral injunctions, pervades the contemporary writings. The heroic deeds that daring individuals undertook in the name of God and king are recounted with a view to obtaining royal largess.[1]

The Chilean conquistadores, according to Agustín Edwards, sought to win "disciples for Christ, glory for Spain and fame and riches for themselves." In doing so, Edwards further observes, they exaggerated their military feats, demonstrated a crusading zeal, manifested an intense devotion to their sovereign, and exhibited a pompous concern for their personal honor.[2]

The history of Spain which helps to explain these characteristics and motivations of the conquistador mentality also contributed to the formation of a unique society in the Spanish American domains that belonged to the Crown of Castile. This society, as Magnus Mörner has remarked, "was created by transferring to the New World the hierarchic, estate-based, corporative society of late medieval Castile and imposing that society upon a multiracial, colonial situation."[3] As the transfer and imposition took place in Chile, the basically white upper levels of the social hierarchy became clearly discernible.

Pedro de Valdivia and his most trusted companions who obtained <u>encomiendas</u> (grants of Indians) from him in the initial phase of the conquest established themselves as the earliest authentic elite in the 1540s. Almost indistinguishable from this small group of conquistadores-<u>encomenderos</u> were several outstanding Europeans, including don Francisco de Irarrázaval y Andía, who arrived in Chile in 1557 with Governor García Hurtado de Mendoza.[4]

As it emerged and developed, the aristocracy was not a closed, static group. Rather it was somewhat fluid and composed of at least two circles or layers that overlapped or joined each other at strategic points. Although some of the distinctions were so subtle that only a contemporary insider would fully understand them, the basic social, economic, and political requirements for membership in the topmost inner circle of patricians are clear enough.

Becoming an encomendero was a sign of social prominence in the sixteenth century, and Indian tribute payable from the <u>pueblos</u> (villages) in labor, produce, or money furnished a source of income. While some of the largest early profits came from employing tributaries in gold mining, members of the encomendero class also became landowners. Peninsulars with grants of Indians very quickly recognized the advantage of owning farms (<u>chacras</u> or <u>chácaras</u>) on the outskirts of a city such as Santiago that needed homegrown provisions. Legal titles to large estates known as <u>estancias</u> and <u>haciendas</u> tended to be acquired more slowly through a series of purchases or gubernatorial land grants that might span more than one generation. Needless to say, some land titles rested on illegal expropriation of Indian holdings. The outcome of the process was the formation of an elite corps of patricians wielding considerable power over the encomienda villagers toiling in the fields, vineyards, pastures, workshops, grain mills, and tanneries that their encomenderos owned. By the early seventeenth century, the term <u>vecinos feudatarios</u> referred to the patrician elite composed of landowning encomenderos who claimed descent from the earliest conquistadores and settlers.[5]

In specific and general laws and decrees (<u>cédulas</u>), the Hapsburg monarchs sought to restrict the exploitation of Indian workers and the expropriation of village lands.[6] The crown nevertheless encouraged and endorsed the elite's social preeminence. A place at the pinnacle of society thus carried political connotations. To acquire and retain membership in the topmost stratum, individuals and, because of the importance of lineage and kinship, their families had to meet certain criteria. These standards emanated from the medieval peninsular experience.

Law and custom had long sanctioned the practice of winning the royal seal of approval for personal and familial status. Echoes of feudalism and the chivalric code of behavior set the tone for the personal ties and reciprocal relationship between the king as feudal lord and his vassals, first in Spain and later in America. As Néstor Meza Villalobos has explained, the king dispensed justice not only in rendering equitable verdicts in court cases but also distributing favors to deserving vassals. In turn, vassals owed fealty and service to the lord who tempered his royal decisions according to the dictates of Christian morality. The king was obliged to "maintain order, peace and justice" in his realms and to manifest "piety, justice and paternal love" while practicing the virtue of "liberality" in bestowing largess. His colonial vassals claimed to be worthy of his benefactions because they were his creditors. They had impoverished themselves and their families through selfless efforts and expenditures in the conquest and settlement of the new lands.[7]

The ideals of peninsular hidalgos and colonial aristocrats closely resemble those that Sidney Painter identifies as the feudal chivalric virtues of military prowess, loyalty, courtesy towards one's peers, generosity, often expressed as hospitality, and a burning ambition for glory.[8] Variations and specific examples of these ideals appear repeatedly in the records known as <u>probanzas</u>, or <u>informaciones</u>, <u>de méritos y servicios</u>.[9] Such documentation was the approved device not only for citing accomplishments to solicit largess but also, in matters of litigation, contrasting one's qualifications with those of an opponent to win a lawsuit (<u>pleito</u>).

Notwithstanding the tendency of colonists to exaggerate their proofs of merits and services, the documents, if used with the necessary caution, can provide biographical data. For example, probanzas pertaining to men who fought in the Araucanian war recreate battle scenes that place an individual in a particular campaign on the southern frontier. While mere skirmishes become major engagements pitting hundreds or even thousands of Indian warriors against woefully out-numbered, valiant Spaniards, the role of Indian allies and black auxiliaries in redressing the balance is for the most part overlooked. The Indians requested for an encomienda in the south or in the Central Valley by a vassal, who had enlarged the royal domains through victories over enormous odds, are uniformly described as too few in number to provide an adequate reward. Informaciones and pleitos are therefore an unreliable demographical guide. Financial data are similarly suspect because expenses and debts are regularly inflated to contrast with the minuscule compensation sought. Since the documentation is laced with superlatives, a healthy skepticism is therefore advisable in regard to military feats, Indian population, and monetary matters. Yet the hyperbole itself offers important clues to the applicant's frame of mind.

Probanzas and pleitos follow a basic pattern consisting of formal permission from the authorities to collect and forward information to the crown, the petitioner's evidence, usually in the form of questions and hence called the <u>interrogatorio</u>, followed by testimony from witnesses on the particular points. Those that weathered the stormy Atlantic and reached the king and his advisers in the Council of the Indies often bear notations about the disposition of the case. In some instances, it is possible to locate the royal cédula containing the king's final ruling.

The crown's willingness to receive and even solicit not only probanzas but also reports from officials and letters from private individuals supports Lewis Hanke's contention that both legal formalism and freedom of expression figured in the climate of opinion in the Hapsburg era.[10] From another standpoint, sending probanzas to the king was somewhat analogous to the modern day practice of submitting professional résumés to an employer.

An aspirant for a reward or a favorable verdict in a court case looked to the past, present, and future. The record of the past stressed the individual's quality (<u>calidad</u>) and recited personal contributions to the crown. Using a carefully contrived argument from poverty, the petitioner spoke of present needs and sought security for the future. The latter almost always mentioned marital and parental responsibilities and sometimes took the form of asking for help in endowing daughters for marriage. Any memorable forebears were called to the king's attention.[11] The emphasis on ancestry stemmed from the fact that merits and services were hereditary.[12]

The hereditary nature of merits and services meant that aristocrats had to give great care to the choice of a marriage partner. The prospective spouse was evaluated in terms of lineage, race, and religion as well as character, financial potential, and standing in the community. Carefully arranged marriages thus became a hallmark of the patriciate and those aspiring to join it. Very soon an intricate web of marital and kinship alliances appeared.[13]

The historical record fortunately preserves papers regarding don Francisco de Irarrázaval, his wife doña Lorenza de Zárate, their children, and their extended family that make it possible to examine these attitudes and practices in further detail. Episodes from their lives provide a framework for chapters 1 and 2 that trace a petition from its inception through complex litigation to the crown's ultimate response in a royal decree. Since language is instructive, textual analysis is used. In chapter 3, family concerns, including land acquisitions and marital alliances, receive attention.

Chapter 1

The Young Cavalier

In 1555 two gentlemen of the royal household of Prince Philip of Spain obtained licenses to sail to the Indies on a ship under the command of Diego Martín. Each of the youthful courtiers who had been born in the 1530s would leave a mark on Chilean history. Don Alonso de Ercilla y Zúñiga's stay in the far southern outpost of the Spanish empire was brief but sufficient to inspire his internationally acclaimed epic <u>La Araucana</u> that extolled the valor of Spaniards and Indians on the military frontier. The other young peninsular was don Francisco de Irarrázaval y Andía whose association with the future sovereign Philip II would prove most fortuitous in consolidating a prestigious position in Chilean society for himself and his descendants.[1]

Don Francisco hailed from a Basque province and descended from individuals who had obtained honors and rewards from the crown of Castile. Although the precise social level of his forebears is difficult to determine, his father, Antón González de Andía Irarrázaval, had inherited property and enjoyed genteel status that devolved upon his heirs. Don Francisco's use of the title don, for example, attests to his rank. While his immigration license identifies his mother as doña María de Aguirre, other sources refer to her as doña María Martínez de Aguirre.[2]

In 1548 don Francisco acquired a place at court as a page to Prince Philip, the son of the Emperor Charles V. He was subsequently promoted to the rank of gentleman (*gentilhombre costiller*) of Philip's household. The young Basque and his elder brother don Menjón, who had also become a courtier, were in the retinue that accompanied the Hapsburg prince to England for his marriage to Queen Mary Tudor in 1554.[3] As the first born son, don Menjón's prospects were considerably better than those of don Francisco. The lessons of court life were nonetheless useful to the latter who had the opportunity to learn at first hand about procedures and protocol. It was at this time, if not before, that don Francisco became acquainted with Ercilla.

Life in the English court took on a heightened excitement when reports arrived from Peru and Chile. Jerónimo de Alderete had returned to Europe on a mission that was threefold: to convey messages and Chilean gold from his friend and companion Pedro de Valdivia to the crown, to help the conquistador's wife doña Marina Ortiz de Gaete and his own wife doña Esperanza de Rueda ready themselves for the voyage to Chile, and to recruit additional colonists. After doña Marina embarked in 1554, news arrived of her husband's death at the hands of the Araucanians, and Alderete stepped forward as a candidate for the vacant governorship. He won the appointment from the Regent, Princess Juana, in 1555. His entourage for the return voyage included his wife, relatives, retainers, and servants. Other parties of emigrants who were enticed by New World opportunities also began to form.[4]

The future poet Ercilla headed one such group bound for Chile and don Francisco de Irarrázaval another. Don Francisco's small following totaled four unmarried men listed on his official passport in 1555 as criados, meaning servants and/or retainers.[5] Four years later he reviewed his experiences at court and his reasons for emigrating. The probanza of merits and services that he prepared in September, 1559, stated that he had served Philip II unerringly since his childhood. Specifically, he was a page and gentilhombre costiller in the kingdoms of Spain. While in England with His Highness, he learned that Francisco Hernández Girón was leading an uprising in Peru against Spanish authority. The document failed to mention that the Peruvian rebels were defeated before he arrived in South America. Instead, it stressed the young gentleman's reaction to the news from Chile where Indians were waging war against Spaniards and had killed Governor Valdivia in the course of their rebellion that forced colonists from their settlements in the south. Don Francisco had therefore resolved to leave his place in the royal household and to go "to that conquest and war."[6]

Don Francisco was probably truthful in recounting his zeal for service, a carefully cultivated aristocratic attribute. Other motives, however, had no doubt also influenced him to try his luck in America. Obtaining a livelihood was surely something to consider. Moreover, the unstable conditions in Chile offered the Basque vassal the opportunity to prove his mettle and win recognition and compensation. His chances of obtaining either would not noticeably improve if he remained in the courtly precincts because his elder brother would take precedence. In any event, Irarrázaval weighed his choices, journeyed from England to Spain, and began the mundane preparations facing any emigrant.

As he made financial arrangements and purchased items necessary for the voyage and for life in a new environment he obtained a license to export goods worth 1,000 pesos free of export duty.[7] While this was a sign of royal approval, don Francisco sought a more explicit endorsement of his merits and services. How much evidence the young courtier could marshal in support of his claim for preferment is unknown. It is quite likely that he cited the probanza his father prepared in 1531 after participating in a peninsular military campaign. The evidence was sufficient, in any case, for Princess Juana to sign a letter of recommendation for him to the governor of Chile on March 5, 1555, in Valladolid. The regent identified don Francisco as a gentleman of Prince Philip's household who was duly licensed to go to Chile to continue serving the crown, as he and his forebears had done in the peninsular kingdoms, and worthy to receive every appropriate "favor" (merced). The governor was to remember him when distributing the "profits" of that land and entrust him with "offices and duties according to the quality of his person."[8] In emigrating from Spain, don Francisco was thus following the family tradition of royal service. He was not effecting a change of career but merely choosing a new locale for his endeavors.

With his valuable letter, small retinue, and necessary supplies, don Francisco was ready to sail from Spain. He was not untypical of other junior members of well-placed families below grandee status who joined the emigrant throngs.

Status and perquisites were nevertheless scant insurance against the perils of sixteenth-century Atlantic crossings. A storm at sea drove the ship carrying the Alderete party back to port for repairs, and later a tropical fever took the new governor's life off the coast of Panamá. Don Francisco thus became one of many colonists headed for Chile deprived of their leader and mentor. A more prestigious official, the newly-appointed Viceroy of Peru, the Marqués de Cañete, don Andrés Hurtado de Mendoza, took charge, however, and named his twenty-two-year-old son acting governor of Chile to replace Alderete. Although nepotism could lead to charges against an official in the judicial review of his conduct known as a residencia, the gentlemen Ercilla and Irarrázaval evidently saw nothing wrong with the appointment. They duly enrolled in the force of approximately 400 men assembled under the command of Governor García Hurtado de Mendoza. The expedition, that also included a number of Spanish women and children, arrived in the Chilean northern district of Coquimbo in April, 1557.[9]

In the three years following the death of Valdivia, the colony had been racked with turmoil. The Araucanians, famed for their military prowess, had regained almost all of their southern homelands as Spanish settlers fled from the war zone to the relative safety of the Central Valley. The influx of refugees from the south put a considerable strain on the small city of Santiago that had been founded in 1541. An Araucanian offensive penetrated the Central Valley and aimed at driving the Spaniards from the capital itself but was turned back in 1557 with the help of Indian auxiliaries known as indios amigos. The political situation had gone from bad to worse with city councils and Valdivia's lieutenants vying for control. The Viceroy Hurtado de Mendoza had hoped to bring order out of chaos by appointing his son to the governorship. Unfortunately, the conditions in Chile called for experience and expertise that were sadly lacking in the youthful governor, who had not yet reached his twenty-fifth birthday, the legal age of majority. As a recent arrival from Spain, the new chief executive had scant knowledge of the ways of the Indies. Don García chose to concentrate on his military role and wanted to win a reputation as the commander who reconquered the south. Time would prove, however, that he, like others before and after him, failed to subdue the Araucanians. His advisers, most notably the licentiate Hernando de Santillán and fray Gil González de San Nicolás, meanwhile strove to defend and advance the cause of the Chilean Indians throughout the colony.[10]

The struggle for justice regarding Indians and their rights is a well known theme in the conquest and colonization of Spanish America, giving it, as Lewis Hanke has observed, a "unique quality" in the history of empire building. During the administration of Hurtado de Mendoza, the struggle began in earnest in Chile and would continue despite the setbacks that his advisers suffered. The crown had assigned Santillán to the high court (audiencia) of Lima as a judge (oidor), and the viceroy sent him to Chile as chief justice. There he drafted ordinances designed to curb the blatant exploitation of Indian workers. Although the legislation ultimately received royal approval, it made few inroads against the labor abuses that encomenderos perpetrated against Indian men, women, and children. Similarly, the efforts of fray Gil González, a Dominican priest, met with little success. Not only the colonists but the governor himself paid scant attention to the ardent friar who advocated defensive tactics and condemned the military conquest of the frontier. Since the governor was determined to restore Spanish dominion over the Araucanians, by force of arms not peaceful persuasion, he wasted little time in setting sail from Coquimbo in June,

1557.[11]

    In the war-torn lands of the south, don Francisco and Ercilla campaigned under Hurtado de Mendoza's command for a little over a year. They helped reestablish the city of Concepción that had been abandoned after Governor Valdivia's death, build forts, found new settlements, fight rebellious Indians, and explore new lands in and near the archipelago that includes the island of Chiloé. Don Francisco's companion at court and in arms mentioned him as a participant in the battles described in La Araucana, the epic that supplements prose sources. The narrative of their activity as presented in don Francisco's probanza of merits and services in 1559, including supporting testimony from Ercilla and other witnesses, correlates well with the sequence of events in contemporary chronicles. The document is strangely silent, however, in regard to the solemnities held in the city of Imperial in 1558 to mark Charles V's abdication in favor of Philip II.[12] Perhaps the frontier observances were too rustic to impress a royal courtier. If don Francisco felt the beauty of the majestic Andes, the verdant valleys, and the blue Pacific, he failed to record his emotions. He was, in any case, preparing a petition not a travelog, and it was his friend Ercilla who had the soul of a poet.

    Don Francisco initiated the probanza in Lima to file a claim for compensation befitting his quality, service, and financial expenditures. Since it met the requirements set by law and the royal audiencia that performed both administrative and judicial functions, it would be forwarded to the king and the Council of the Indies in Spain for action. The petitioner accordingly addressed himself to His Highness, reminding Philip II that he had been in the royal household and emigrated from Spain after learning of the Indian rebellion in Chile and obtaining a letter of recommendation to the Chilean governor. Upon arriving in Peru, he kept his "arms and horses and trappings" in good order and joined the viceregal retinue.[13]

He accompanied Governor García Hurtado de Mendoza to Chile as a "caballero" who was well equipped with "weapons and horses" and two Spanish criados. In northern Chile, he had gone into debt to purchase more supplies for himself and his two men who would serve in the war with him. When the governor's forces reached the southern Araucanian country, they were buffeted by a storm at sea and camped on an island near the deserted city of Concepción where hardships and hunger compounded the burdens of bearing arms and standing sentry duty. After two months, the governor sent don Francisco in an advance column to build a fort on the mainland. Not only his personal attendants but he himself labored on the construction project in that war zone. They worked together later in helping to build a fort in the valley of Tucapel near the new city of Cañete, and he boasted that he did more work than anyone else.

According to don Francisco the long trek from the city of Valdivia to the southern archipelago was often literally a march, because horses could not make their way through the bogs and across the rivers. The chronicler Pedro Mariño de Lobera added that the heavily wooded area made it necessary to use axes and machetes to cut a path through the thickets and thorny branches.[14] The witness Ercilla remembered that food ran low.

The native islanders were not particularly hostile, but Araucanians time and again disputed the Spanish efforts to reoccupy their lands. On these occasions, don Francisco assured Philip II, he fought well and bravely, never holding back. He placed himself in grave danger, risking his life in the perils of battle as a caballero should. The Araucanians thus supplied Ercilla with material for his epic and don Francisco with the opportunity to win his spurs and boast of it in his probanza. The witness Diego de Llanos, who testified in the latter's behalf, confirmed that he was a good fighting man but was not sure that he was correct in claiming to be among the first to break the Indian squadrons at Tucapel.

Irarrázaval concluded his probanza in September, 1559, with a résumé of his most recent activities. He had spent some months in 1558 with the governor in Imperial and became convinced that the war was over. Since the pacification had been successful, there was no further military service to perform for the crown in Chile. He therefore obtained the governor's permission to return to Lima to apply for his reward. He lodged in the viceroy's house, according to the witness Francisco de Ulloa, who cited this as evidence of genteel stature. Now deeply in debt, don Francisco asserted that he needed one of the best Chilean encomiendas to pay his debts and support himself like a servant of the king.

Several points in the document deserve consideration. For example, don Francisco's abrupt departure from Chile where competition over encomiendas was already acute[15] occurred in a mood of disappointment since his letter of royal recommendation had not produced any immediate and tangible favor. Did he also surmise from the talk around the campfires and in the tiny Spanish settlements that the military campaigns would not long subdue the Araucanian resistance that his poet-friend immortalized? If so, an ambitious yet prudent young man might well declare the military operations successful and take advantage of the lull in the fighting to retire from active duty and seek a safer, more comfortable haven in Peru.

The probanza is true to form in extolling don Francisco as a caballero both for his unremitting service--in fighting, working, suffering, and impoverishing himself for the king--and his quality as a gentleman who employed retainers and attached himself to the viceregal court. While others might speak of any horsemen as caballeros, the petitioner characterized himself as a cavalier in the more restricted meaning of the term: he fought like a knight and conducted himself like a gentleman. The association with the viceroy, the king's alter ego, signified his social status. Moreover, it showed that his early experience as a royal courtier had taught him the practical value of proximity to high places. The document aptly portrays the courtly gentleman who armed himself as a knight, a mounted warrior, in the name of his royal lord yet maintained a realistic concern for his own material advancement.

Other terms also carry important connotations. Governor Hurtado de Mendoza's campaign is described as conquest and war against rebel Indians. But the document also speaks of pacification, a word that became an official substitute for conquest. The change in language was a small step in the Spanish struggle for justice regarding Indian servitude and the nature of a "just war."[16] Although both matters were being aired during the Hurtado de Mendoza administration,[17] the probanza indicates that don Francisco gave little thought to the arguments propounded and the policies enacted in Chile. For example, quelling rebellious Indians is depicted as a praiseworthy endeavor undertaken in behalf of the king. Most of the battles are described as defensive actions to repel attacks. Even the invasion of the Indian lands of Arauco and Tucapel was launched as a "punishment." In the context of the document, the Indians deserved this chastisement for prior offenses against the Spaniards in the south. These oblique references to the justice of the conquest reveal that don Francisco was not overly troubled by the finer points of the debate on whether war against the Indians was illicit or morally defensible. From his point of view, Indian servitude needed no rationalization at all. He made a straightforward request for a grant of Indians because he believed his merits and services made him a worthy candidate for the encomendero class. He took for granted the notion of an aristocracy drawing support from servile labor.

Don Francisco was not yet ready to return to Chile, however. Instead he went to Spain to lobby for royal largess in person. To reenforce the probanza, he secured a letter of recommendation from the viceroy to the king on October 28, 1559. The marqués de Cañete wrote that don Francisco de Irarrázaval had served in pacifying, colonizing, and settling Chile until all this was accomplished. He showed himself to be a "caballero and prudent and of good habits," and thus a credit to his upbringing in His Majesty's household. He had now decided to come to Spain and report directly to the king. As a person, he was qualified for any favor that the crown would deem appropriate.[18] Don Francisco's association with the Hurtado de Mendoza father and son who headed the Peruvian and Chilean administrations was obviously paying dividends.

The would-be encomendero encountered few if any delays in making his way to court and obtaining a hearing. On February 19, 1561, he secured a royal decree commending him to the new viceroy of Peru and ordering that official to asist the king's "gentilhombre" if he should spend any time when passing through Peru to Chile.[19]

An entrée of this type was not especially noteworthy, but don Francisco had already won a more important reward from his royal patron. The Council of the Indies had endorsed his petition for an encomienda and submitted it to Philip II, who granted the request in a royal cédula directed to the governor of Chile on January 22, 1561.[20] This decree is significant, in the first place, because it had an immediate bearing on don Francisco's career. Few colonists had the wherewithal to elicit such direct royal aid. Secondly, it repeats concepts stated in his probanza and thereby illustrates that the mutual expectations of king and cavalier coincided. The document, which follows the stylized conventions of decrees bestowing largess, is thus a prime example of the attitudes and reciprocal relationship that the Hapsburg monarchs and aristocratic colonists shared. The decree and the probanza are representative of the interchanges between peninsular lord and colonial vassal who spoke the same chivalric language.

Philip II's decree, signed with the formal "I the King," summarized the events that had transpired after don Francisco de Irarrázaval, a gentleman of his household, had obtained royal permission to accompany Governor Alderete to Chile some seven years earlier. Since Alderete died en route, don Francisco joined the

García Hurtado de Mendoza expedition. He was "very well prepared with horses and arms and took with him two servants," who would "serve together with him." Since the Indians were rebelling, he helped "in the pacification" of the land. He always found himself in the "forefront" of battle and did what "our good and faithful servant and vassal was obliged to do." After the Indians were subdued and "brought to peace," he participated in the discovery of "other lands and provinces" in Chile. In all of this, he experienced "great hardships and necessities and put his person in much risk." Moreover, he spent "much of his wealth and patrimony" on these activities. Don Francisco wanted to return to Chile "to serve us...as he has done until now." He has petitioned me, Philip II continued, to command that he be given one of the better, unclaimed grants of Indians located in the jurisdictional limits of Santiago or Concepción, that would yield an annual income of ten or twelve thousand gold pesos "in remuneration of his services." He wanted the encomienda in order "to support himself honorably in accordance with the quality of his person." Since the Council of the Indies, after studying the request and the information from the probanza, had recommended a favorable response from the sovereign, the king acknowledged the role of the Council, accepted the advice, and ordered the governor to confer an encomienda upon don Francisco befitting "his services and the quality of his person." The decree, which stopped short of specifying a monetary value for the grant, thus left to the governor's discretion how many Indians don Francisco would need to support himself. Philip II, known as the Prudent King, did however stipulate that the encomienda was to be "vacant" or selected from the first ones to fall vacant. (This terminology meant, of course, that the Irarrázaval grant should not be taken from another person.) The king further commanded that don Francisco must abide by "the conditions and duties" that applied to the other Chilean encomenderos.[21]

Don Francisco evidently had little difficulty in complying with the law requiring encomenderos to be married householders.[22] He and his wife would eventually establish their home in Santiago, and it is possible that he and doña Lorenza de Zárate, the daughter of don Diego Ortiz de Zárate and doña María de Recalde, were already betrothed, if not man and wife, when Philip II issued the encomienda decree. Given the attitudes and practices of the day, careful negotiations no doubt preceded the marriage contract, but Chilean historians and genealogists have not yet discovered the terms of the agreement or the value of the dowry, which by law equaled a daughter's parental inheritance. They have established, however, that the wedding took place in the early 1560s in Seville. It was there that doña Lorenza's father had served as an official (contador) in the House of Trade. His position in that government agency and knighthood in the Order of Santiago,[23] indicate that doña Lorenza came from a reputable family.

Although the newlyweds obtained a license to emigrate with doña Lorenza's brother, don Fernando de Zárate, and three servants in March, 1562, the first indication of their presence in Peru dates from June, 1563. On November 10, don Francisco informed Philip II, in a letter to the Council of the Indies, of recent events. I arrived here in Lima, he said, with my wife and household in June, 1563. While I was preparing to go to Chile to obtain my encomienda, bad news arrived. The letter went on to explain that Governor Francisco de Villagra (who replaced Hurtado de Mendoza) had died soon after his son was killed in an Indian rebellion. During his last illness, the governor had named his relative Pedro de Villagra as his interim successor. The viceroy then confirmed the provisional governorship, commissioned Irarrázaval to deliver the appointment, and gave him 1,600 gold pesos from the royal treasury to defray expenses, with the proviso that he had to secure royal authorization for the payment within three years. If he failed to do so, he would have to repay the money and thus he thought it wise to explain the hardships the mission would entail. He would travel overland across dangerous territory which perforce required him to take men with him and incur heavy expenses. Since the route was too long and hazardous for his wife and household, he would have to return later to accompany her by sea. He not only accepted the mission and spent the 1,600 pesos in the king's service but also invested much of his own money in preparing for the expedition. Therefore, he wanted the king to endorse the payment he had received from the Peruvian treasury office.[24] Mixing personal information and official business in a communiqué of this type was not at all unusual because colonists regarded the king both as their sovereign and a caring paternal figure.

Don Francisco's departure from Lima marked the first of several physical separations that doña Lorenza had to face during her marriage. Her brother don Fernando probably stayed with her but may have been too young to be of much help. Nor is it likely that her first cousin don Juan Ortiz de Zárate was on hand to lend aid and comfort. This relative, who had been in Peru for over twenty years, had his own career to pursue in Charcas (modern Bolivia). It is nevertheless possible that he had friends and associates in Lima who were ready to lend doña Lorenza a hand or money should she need either while she adjusted to the rapid changes in her life.[25] Reaching out for help would not be a sign of weakness but a normal human response from a person who had recently married and crossed the Atlantic to an alien land.

When her husband reached Chile, he obtained a writ of encomienda from provisional Governor Pedro de Villagra on September 2, 1564. It was necessary to justify any such benefice, and the governor marshalled the evidence. There were the familiar references to the candidate's stature as a courtier, caballero, and person of quality as well as his prior service in Chile. This worthy individual had recently returned from Spain with his "wife and children, servants, household and family."[26] The reference to offspring supports genealogical sources that indicate one or more of the Irarrázaval y Zárate children were baptized in Peru;[27] unfortunately, Villagra's statement does not help to establish the birthdates.

Since the writ of encomienda responded to the royal cédula of 1561, the text of the decree was incorporated. Following this, Villagra gave a brief history of the Quillota encomienda that was located in the Central Valley, to explain why he chose to entrust those Indians to don Francisco. The encomienda had pertained to don Rodrigo González Marmolejo, the first bishop of Santiago. Recently, the audiencia of Lima had asserted the crown's direct rights over the Indians. To comply with the court order, Governor Villagra had placed the royal treasury officials in possession of the encomienda and appointed Irarrázaval to administer it because those officials had a poor record when they were in charge of it previously. They had diverted the encomienda income and the personal service of the Indians to their own uses, leaving His Majesty little if any profit. Furthermore, they lacked a proprietary interest in the well-being of the Indians, injured them, and caused them to decrease in numbers. It was better, in Villagra's opinion, for "conquistadores and settlers" to receive encomiendas, at least until Chile was totally pacified. He therefore conferred the Quillota encomienda, in the name of the king, on don Francisco de Irarrázaval, with the enjoinder to present final royal approval within three year's time or forfeit all tribute and income he had received. As an encomendero, he was obliged to assume the following responsibilities. (1) He was to observe the royal commands and ordinances regarding the good treatment, conservation, and increase of the Indians and (2) instruct them in the Catholic faith, natural law, and good conduct; any failures in these matters would weigh not on the king's or the governor's conscience, but on his. (3) He had to follow any tribute regulations (<u>tasas</u>) in effect during his tenure as an encomendero or be subject to the penalties set in the tasas. (4) The encomendero had to supply himself with weapons and horses and be ready for active duty during rebellions and (5) see to the repairs of bridges and roads within the encomienda's locale. These duties and the injunction to obtain royal confirmation of the grant were standard features in writs of encomienda.[28]

The routine nature of the writ should not disguise the fundamental significance of its contents. Ideally and legally the encomendero's rights to Indian tribute were supposed to be limited and balanced by his role in military defense and assumption of the responsibility for converting and caring for the Indian wards that Villagra entrusted to him, pending the final nod of approval from Philip II.

Irarrázaval lost little time in taking possession of the grant. This was a formal yet personal ceremony enacted between the encomendero and two Indians representing the headmen (caciques) from Quillota before the deputy governor and chief justice of Santiago and three witnesses. A notary recorded this legal step on September 9, 1564.[29]

Since the new encomendero needed royal confirmation of his grant, he hurried to Lima, secured notarized copies of the writ and act of possession, and forwarded the originals to Spain in November, 1564. With the papers went his power of attorney to his widowed mother-in-law, doña María de Recalde, and several men, some in high offices, authorizing them to seek the necessary approval from the king. Irarrázaval further charged them to petition for additional remuneration of his services in the form of offices and encomiendas.[30]

Don Francisco also sent a covering letter to Philip II on November 20, 1564, reporting on his affairs and Chilean conditions. He had acted as Governor Pedro de Villagra's messenger, he said, to bring the word that Chile needed reinforcements and war materiél from Peru. Since leaving Spain, don Francisco himself had accumulated personal debts in excess of 12,000 pesos in serving His Highness. With a wife and children to support, he requested royal confirmation of the Quillota encomienda, that was not sufficient of itself to fulfill the decree of 1561. He therefore expected more Indians to be entrusted to him. Meanwhile, Governor Villagra had granted him an annual stipend from the Chilean treasury to meet necessities. Don Francisco asked the king to authorize the payment from the royal mining tax (<u>quinto</u> <u>real</u>) rather than revenue from Indian tribute because there was little monetary tribute in the treasury. There were three reasons for this: (1) Chilean Indians rendered personal service instead of paying tribute in money, (2) at present there were no tributaries under direct royal administration, and (3) unless Philip II took action against the practice of transferring encomiendas, none would escheat to the crown.[31]

The last point led don Francisco into a diatribe against the then quasi-legal procedure known as <u>dejación</u>. An encomendero whose writ was due to expire when he died would select a new candidate for the grant and, in connivance with the governor, renounce the encomienda in favor of the new beneficiary. As examples, don Francisco cited encomenderos who transferred encomiendas for some private gain and others who used their grants to endow their <u>mestiza</u> (female Euro-Indian) daughters for marriage to newcomers to Chile.[32] What he did not explain was that the dejación process was also a stratagem for prolonging encomienda titles beyond two generations.[33]

Don Francisco was nevertheless aware of the law of "two lives" that allowed the widow of an encomendero to inherit the grant in the absence of legitimate male or female offspring.[34] He accordingly explained to Philip II how unmarried Chilean encomenderos misused the legal prerogative. When these men felt death approaching, they married in haste to prevent their encomiendas from escheating to crown. Since the brides were often their female slaves, these <u>esclavas</u> <u>moriscas</u> and other women of low estate (<u>mujeres</u> <u>bajas</u>) became <u>encomenderas</u> (females holding grants of Indians).[35] If don Francisco had named the offenders who entered deathbed marriages, as many were accused of doing in the Indies, it might be possible to decipher what he meant by calling the slaves "moriscas." Although Philip II in Spain would understand him to mean that they were Christians of Muslim descent, the term carried other connotations in South America that alluded to skin color or African birth.[36]

While the letter betrayed bias against mestizas and moriscas, the remarks derived not only from social and ethnic considerations but also the correspondent's ambitions to acquire more Indians and to accentuate his qualifications for the largess he sought. If the king were not concerned about the social consequences of dejaciones, perhaps he could be moved to action by an exposé of the baneful political and military effects that resulted when unworthy Chileans "usurped" encomiendas that should have reverted to the crown. This diminished not only the king's authority but also the royal patrimony and therefore proved prejudicial to candidates for encomiendas who had earned merits for rewards in Chile. They became discouraged, avoided the war, and hence Indian rebellions went unrepulsed.[37]

This doleful account did not prompt immediate legislation against the practice of transferring encomiendas, and don Francisco's personal knowledge of its effects, as we shall see, soon increased. Whether he received the financial stipend from the Chilean treasury remains a moot question. Since Pedro de Villagra left office in 1565, it is possible that the new provisional Governor, Rodrigo de Quiroga, disallowed the payments before Irarrázaval began to receive his annuity.

The historical record is nonetheless quite clear on the king's answer to the request for confirmation of the Quillota encomienda title. The reply came in a royal decree dated August 7, 1565, ordering those Indians placed under direct royal control for the immediate future. Philip II tempered this ruling, however, by commanding that don Francisco de Irarrázaval should be entrusted with a different, vacant encomienda in accordance with the previous decree of 1561.[38]

The king's ruling represented a predictable compromise, not entirely unprofitable to Philip II and rather favorable to his courtier, in the course of protracted litigation over the Quillota encomienda. The final verdict went against don Francisco and restored the encomienda to a previous holder, Juan Gómez, a member of the original conquistador elite; however, the decree of 1565, by reaffirming the earlier cédula, no doubt proved helpful to don Francisco in eventually obtaining a new grant.[39]

The trials, in both a literal and a figurative sense, of getting and keeping an encomienda are the subject of the next chapter.

Chapter 2

In Quest of Rewards

When candidates for the same encomienda sued each other, the litigation was essentially a contest between rivals pleading their cases for a royal favor. Each litigant submitted documented evidence of merits and services and measured it against the opponent's record. A pleito thus featured the same type of data found in a probanza but added charges to demean and discredit the opponent. The king, working with the Council of the Indies, acted as the final arbitrator in substantial civil suits that could not be resolved in the colonies. The crown's ultimate sovereignty over the Amerindians in the overseas realms meant that the monarch either personally with the Council of the Indies, or through his colonial courts, exercised royal jurisdiction over encomienda cases with a view to the well-being of the Indians to be awarded to the litigant with the better claim on the royal patrimony. A _fiscal_ (crown attorney) might represent the king's interest in a particular suit, as occurred in the

Irarrázaval vs. Gómez case involving the Quillota encomienda.

The crown's immediate interest in the Quillota litigation stemmed from the fact that the encomienda had twice come under direct royal control in a series of allocations and reallocations that were more complex than the summary view that acting Governor Pedro de Villagra presented in don Francisco's writ. Pedro de Valdivia had initially reserved the Quillota Indians for himself but later entrusted them to don Rodrigo González Marmolejo, who became the first bishop of Santiago. The audiencia of Lima on March 17, 1555, asserted the crown's direct rights over the encomienda, citing one of the famous New Laws of 1542 and a subsequent royal decree of 1551 which together prohibited civil officials and clergymen from becoming encomenderos. Governor Hurtado de Mendoza implemented the court order by placing the Quillota encomienda in the hands of the royal treasury officials in Santiago. Lengthy investigations--including one conducted by the licentiate Hernando de Santillán, in his capacity as chief justice of Chile--returned a telling indictment of their conduct as Indian agents. They responded with an impressive defense, however. In the course of the proceedings, testimony for and against the treasury officials was taken from both Indians and Spaniards. For example, an Indian headman prepared a sworn statement with the help of a mestizo interpreter, and fray Gil González de San Nicolás, the Dominican priest, submitted a deposition. Governor

Hurtado de Mendoza finally ruled against the treasury officials who had obviously failed to convince him that either the royal coffers or the Indians benefited from their administrative practices.[1] He therefore granted the encomienda to Juan Gómez on December 31, 1560.[2]

Gómez nevertheless lost the Quillota Indians to the bishop who regained control of them shortly before he died. Governor Francisco de Villagra had implemented the transfer and soon bestowed the encomienda on Diego Mazo de Alderete, a newcomer in Chile. The Lima high court again intervened, voiding the Mazo de Alderete grant and ordering the Indians restored to royal control. Provisional Governor Pedro de Villagra duly conferred possession of the encomienda on the treasury officials and appointed Irarrázaval to administer the Indians. Later he saw fit to remove the treasury officials from the picture and, as we have seen, issued a writ of encomienda to don Francisco in 1564.[3]

These multiple transfers took place amid the inevitable claims and counterclaims of the candidates vying for control and were further complicated by transfers of other Indians and more lawsuits. The allegations and protests repeat the familiar refrain of too few Indians to distribute among the many aspirants to encomendero status. For instance, a witness commented in 1565 that Chile was "such a poor land" and had so "few natives" that there was little with which "to gratify" those who had served there.[4]

Who were these individuals seeking gratification

from the crown and competing with Irarrázaval for the encomienda that represented both a source of livelihood and a symbol of social distinction? The litigation documents fortunately provide rather satisfactory answers regarding the litigants, their positions in society, and their activities during the period of conquest and early settlement.

As a young man, Diego Mazo de Alderete participated in a voyage through the Strait of Magellan to reconnoiter the Chilean coast but resided in the colony only briefly during the Francisco and Pedro de Villagra administrations. There he married a sister to doña Cándida de Montesa, Governor Francisco de Villagra's wife. The marriage to doña María de Espinosa and the writ of encomienda for the Quillota Indians coincided closely enough for the grant to be denounced, as it soon was, as an act of nepotism. In the later stages of the litigation, don Francisco de Irarrázaval and Juan Gómez contended that Mazo de Alderete lacked the requisite service record in Chile to be awarded an encomienda in that land.[5] While some colonists would look beyond Chile for rewards, tying compensation to the area where service was performed did, in fact, have precedents dating back to the early conquest period.[6] Although he lost the Quillota encomienda, Mazo de Alderete finally obtained the right to a royal pension drawn from Indian tribute in Peru as a reward for his loyalty and service to the king in both Chile and Peru.[7]

Don Francisco, who emphasized Mazo de Alderete's late arrival in Chile, was at a distinct disadvantage when his own brief experience in the Chilean war was compared with that of Juan Gómez, a relative of Diego de Almagro, the leader of the first, disappointing Spanish reconnaissance expedition in Chile. Gómez, who neither titled himself don nor affixed "de Almagro" to his surname, entered Chile with Pedro de Valdivia in 1541, obtained writs of encomienda from the conquistador, belonged to the Santiago city council (cabildo), and held the post of alguacil mayor (chief constable). His most important claim to renown, however, stemmed from leading "The Famous Fourteen" (Los catorce de la fama) in the Araucanian country at the time of Valdivia's death.[8] This episode and how he came to be in the south were grist for the judicial mill in his several lawsuits against Irarrázaval and others.

According to the litigation records, Gómez left Santiago for the southern frontier in 1553. There he exchanged his encomienda, called variously Topocalma and Rapel, in the Central Valley for one in Imperial that belonged to the encomendero Gaspar Orense. Governor Valdivia authorized these renunciations and transfers in November of that year. The two men also traded their livestock, urban and rural real estate, crops, and yanaconas (Indian servitors permanently attached to a household). In a postscript to the notarized bill of exchange, Gómez stated that Orense gave him 200 hens and listed household effects and tools that the latter would receive in Santiago along with salt pork, 100 brood sows with their litters, 35 boars, and a poultry flock of 200 large hens plus 400 assorted hens and capons; but Orense could have the baby chicks without counting them. Since Orense suffered from asthma, according to his former neighbor Juana Jiménez, he was no doubt relieved to learn that he would not have to scamper around tallying baby chicks. Juana, who testified in a lawsuit over the Rapel encomienda, connected his poor health with his desire to go to Santiago and his willingness to trade a much larger encomienda for the smaller one Gómez held.[9]

In the same suit, Gómez gave a terse account of the fateful days in December, 1553. He had gone to Imperial to obtain the Orense encomienda when news came of a revolt, and the city magistrates sent him to the fort of Purén as the "caudillo." After routing Indian attackers, he set out in a party of fourteen horsemen in search of Governor Valdivia at Tucapel only to learn that the Indians had killed him and his men. The survivors, including Gómez, although badly wounded made their way to Concepción.[10] It was this action that earned Juan Gómez, the conquistador turned chicken farmer, a place in the sixteenth-century chronicles as a military leader, a distinction denied don Francisco de Irarrázaval.[11]

In the course of the lawsuits, statements for and against Gómez modified the original story. There were also comments on his activities under Francisco de Villagra who assumed command in the south after Valdivia's death. A writ restoring the Rapel encomienda to Gómez on September 3, 1561, is a case in point. The document, which was admitted into evidence during the litigation, mentioned that his horse was killed in the battle near Tucapel, and he only escaped death himself by hiding from the Araucanians. During the next two years, he fought and contributed to the war effort like "a good soldier" and "loyal vassal," according to Villagra who issued the writ during his term as governor.[12]

The writ was a step toward victory for Gómez in his on-going lawsuits. The hazards of the frontier war convinced him that he had made a terrible mistake in leaving Santiago. His change of residence had occurred just prior to the devastating hostilities that wreaked havoc in the south after Tucapel and prompted his eventual return to the relative peace and stability of the Central Valley. He would spend years reestablishing himself as an encomendero in Santiago.

Unfortunately for Gómez, Governor Hurtado de Mendoza had granted the Rapel encomienda to the conquistador Antonio Tarabajano in 1558 because it fell vacant when Orense died in a shipwreck on his way to Spain. Tarabajano and Gómez then sued each other for possession of Rapel.[13] With Antonio Tarabajano's entry on the scene, the list of parties to the litigation involving don Francisco de Irarrázaval, Juan Gómez, the treasury officials, and the crown attorney is complete.

The Tarabajano-Gómez suit turned largely on the legality of the Rapel renunciation. Gómez argued that it was illegal because he had relinquished the encomienda under duress, alleging that Governor Valdivia forced him to give up the Rapel villagers. Tarabajano maintained that his opponent took the step freely and hence the renunciation in favor of Orense, now deceased, was valid. To prove title to the encomienda, Tarabajano produced his writ from Governor Hurtado de Mendoza.[14]

A further complication arose in the already tangled mass of claims after Tarabajano renounced his encomienda of Gualemo in favor of his son-in-law Agustín Briceño. When Gómez sought title to those Indians, Tarabajano responded in 1565 that they were quite distinct from the Rapel villagers, who were at issue in the suit.[15]

Some two years earlier Gómez had married doña Francisca de Escobedo, the daughter of the licentiate Juan de Escobedo and doña Ursula de Orozco.[16] It is therefore not surprising that Gómez entrusted his father-in-law, who was trained in the law, with his power of attorney to collect further evidence when the Rapel case was appealed to the Council of the Indies. Escobedo tried to impeach the Rapel renunciation on the grounds that a notary, rather than Governor Valdivia's official secretary, recorded it. He also impugned Tarabajano's personal morals by calling witnesses to testify that Tarabajano used the Gualemo encomienda in the marriage dowry for his mestiza daughter born of his adulterous union with an Indian woman. The questions emphasizing Francisca de Tarabajano's illegitimate birth were meant to demean her husband's status and went on to criticize Briceño, a recent arrival in Chile, for lacking any service in that land except that of his work as a notary for an ecclesiastic.[17]

Perhaps Irarrázaval had this case in mind when he condemned encomienda transfers to husbands of mestizas in his letter to the king in 1564. In any event, the contrast between Tarabajano, the adulterer, whose son-in-law followed a sedentary, civilian career and the records on Gómez' active life as an Indian fighter could speak for itself in the halls of justice. It was best to maintain a discreet silence, as Escobedo did, on the fact that Gómez himself had a liaison with an Indian noblewoman (palla) from Peru who accompanied him to Chile and bore him a son.[18]

Antonio Tarabajano of course had both evidence and backers to support his claims to the Rapel Indians. For example, Juan Beltrán de Magaña frankly admitted that he favored Tarabajano over Gómez when he testified in the latter's suit with Irarrázaval concerning the Quillota encomienda.[19]

Beltrán, one of the most open and informative, if opinionated, witnesses in the entire proceedings made his deposition for don Francisco in December, 1565, when the audiencia of Lima was compiling testimony to forward to Spain on a questionnaire Irarrázaval presented. Don Francisco was pleading his case for the Quillota encomienda against Juan Gómez, who had filed suit for it. He also wanted to demonstrate that the crown should not let the treasury officials assume control of the Indians. At this time, he had been in possession of the Quillota encomienda for a year and received income from it by virtue of the writ from provisional Governor Pedro de Villagra, who now testified in his behalf, swearing that he issued the title to comply with the royal decree of 1561. The Rapel encomienda, on the other hand, still belonged to Juan Gómez whose father-in-law was handling it for him.[20]

As the testimony began, Villagra quite logically reaffirmed his previous criticism of the treasury officials. Juan Beltrán declared that Villagra did a "very great service to God and to His Majesty and unburdened the royal conscience" when he stripped the treasury officials of their authority over the Quillota Indians and granted the encomienda to don Francisco. Another witness, Arias Pardo Maldonado, referred to his previous inspection of Indian affairs and suggested that the file should be consulted. It would show that Indians under treasury office administration were treated worse than encomienda Indians whose encomenderos directed and looked after them because they had a greater individual interest in Indian survival. Don Francisco's witnesses also indicated that the treasury officials used Indians for their own profit instead of remitting large tribute payments to the royal treasury. The Quillota Indians were said to number between 150 and 200, another indication that the king would not gain much in terms of revenue if he reclaimed the encomienda. Don

Francisco, on the other hand, stood to lose his only means of support. Villagra thought the income from three encomiendas like Quillota would be insufficient for a man of don Francisco's status; Beltrán asserted that five such grants would not be enough to meet the plaintiff's needs and stature.[21]

In posing the questions for his witnesses, don Francisco had deliberately raised the issue of social status. He repeated the litany featured earlier in his probanza regarding his experience as a royal page and his roles as a cavalier both in the king's household and on the Chilean battlefields where he and two attendants served at his own expense. Don Francisco, the "caballero hijodalgo," added proud references not only to his wife doña Lorenza de Zárate but also to his father and father-in-law. Now with children to support, his only reward for his services and expenditures on behalf of the king was the Quillota encomienda, small in size and low in profits.[22]

Witnesses verified this picture of a worthy, indebted encomendero forced to live in genteel poverty, a condition scarcely befitting his high social rank and that of his wife. The latter, García de Alvarado remarked, was a "very renowned lady." Juan Beltrán also commented on her distinction and the expenses that a prestigious family incurred.[23]

This evidence was designed to appeal to the king's liberality and justice. It rested on the accepted premise that ladies and gentlemen were entitled to maintain an affluent lifestyle reflecting their place in society. In this case, royal approval of the encomienda would provide the Irarrázaval y Zárate family, of proven substance, with the financial means to keep up appearances.

Don Francisco's lineage and position in the king's household, plus his marriage to a gentlewoman whose father had belonged to the Order of Santiago and held an office in the House of Trade, gave him strong leverage against his adversary Juan Gómez. To win a favorable verdict from the king, the royal courtier needed to emphasize that he was more worthy than Gómez.

Questions and testimony accordingly dealt with the financial and social standing of Juan Gómez. Did the witnesses know, don Francisco asked, that Gómez, in terms of his service to the crown, was "more remunerated than any other man" in Chile? Did the Rapel encomienda profit him over 200,000 gold pesos when he first had it and despoiled the Indians? Did he then obtain the large encomienda in Imperial? Did Gómez, "according to his person, house, and family," now have sufficient support from the Rapel encomienda because it currently yielded him 3,000 gold pesos, not counting his other enterprises?[24]

The answers understandably varied on this range of topics, but there was general agreement that Rapel had paid well during the early years of gold mining. Arias Pardo Maldonado, citing his earlier inspection in Chile, stated that the Rapel villagers, in addition to working in Gómez' household, had previously mined over 50,000 gold pesos for him. Antonio Díaz Vera pointed out, however, that war and hunger killed the Indians in Imperial before Gómez had much profit from them. Although the Rapel encomienda population was admittedly diminished, Diego García Altamirano thought it could still produce 3,000 gold pesos per year because other small encomiendas did so.[25]

Juan Beltrán volunteered a lengthy response to the set of questions. He attributed the population decline not only to mining, that earned Gómez 100,000 gold pesos before he renounced Rapel for the southern encomienda, but also to farm work. Thus Gómez had been well rewarded because others with as much seniority in Chilean service had not enjoyed one-tenth of his profits. Nor had they used up and killed so many Indians as Gómez did in Imperial. Rapel alone, however, could not support Gómez, his wife and child, and her parents because the "ostentation" practiced in these parts cost a great deal. Even if Gómez had Rapel, with its 150 Indians, the Quillota encomienda, and still others, he would be unable to pay his debts that exceeded 10,000 pesos, and his income would fall short of what he and his family spent and wasted.[26]

Data on income and lifestyle routinely appeared in encomienda lawsuits. The object in this context was to show that Gómez was well paid for his services and had many valuable Indians entrusted to him. In spite of this, he squandered his income by living above his social station. While it was perfectly appropriate for don Francisco and doña Lorenza to flaunt their acknowledged rank, it was totally unsuitable for the Gómez-Escobedo family members to assume aristocratic ways and reap compensation disproportionate to their status. Let the king note the differences between the encomienda claimants.

Juan Gómez stood beneath don Francisco on the social ladder, and he knew it. His wife was respectable but no match for doña Lorenza. Although Gómez could not prefix his name with don, he ranked above the plebian level and therefore identified himself as an hidalgo. This designation went unchallenged.[27] When Gómez began to style himself "captain," however, both Irarrázaval and Mazo de Alderete called him to account.[28]

The evidence don Francisco assembled turned on the definition of the term. Gómez was not and never claimed to be a captain in the regular army, but on occasion he did command small groups of men. As Diego García Altamirano put it, some people referred to Gómez as captain and others did not. Antonio Díaz Vera's testimony furnished a good example of this. Although he had used the military title in an earlier deposition favorable to Gómez, he now admitted that all he could say was that "they called" Gómez "captain." Juan Beltrán, never one to equivocate, had a definite view of the connotations of that rank and refused to accord it to Gómez. Beltrán, perhaps in deference to the great captains of the conquest of the likes of Cortés in Mexico and Valdivia in Chile, did not consider men who held some brief assignment to be captains. They were merely "caudillos," temporary leaders whose commission expired when the task was accomplished. Arias Pardo Maldonado was equally firm in asserting that he never knew Gómez to have the rank of captain or the command of men during the administrations of Hurtado de Mendoza and Francisco de Villagra; during the latter's governorship, Gómez ignored the need for fighting men and stayed in Santiago where it was as peaceful as the city of Valladolid in Spain.[29]

In building his case, Juan Gómez emphasized his entire residency in Chile, not just the more recent periods and administrations. He drew attention to himself as a sturdy married householder with some 26 years of service that had consumed all his encomienda income, leaving him in debt for over 20,000 pesos. He was a "valiant man" who not only fought brilliantly in person and furnished "many caballeros and hijosdalgos" with lodging, food, clothing, horses, and weapons but also "paid their debts and freight charges." Witnesses confirmed these points to explain how Gómez came to need the Quillota encomienda to supplement Rapel.[30] Don Francisco had depicted him as a wastrel, but Gómez and his friends portrayed a responsible family man whose service to the crown and expenditures on the war effort dated from the Valdivia expedition.

This description called to mind the medieval vassal who kept his retainers in readiness to answer the lord's summons to battle. The characterization of Gómez as a civilian-soldier-settler supporting horsemen needed on the military frontier was also quite true to life in sixteenth-century Chile. A more or less regular subsidy was not available to pay soldiers and purchase supplies for the Araucanian war until the seventeenth century.[31] Conquistadores and early settlers therefore furnished much of the money, materiél, and manpower for the military campaigns. A list of their contributions, usually citing marriage and parenthood as a sign of stability and always underscoring financial hardship, thus became standard in appeals to the crown in both lawsuits and probanzas.[32]

While Gómez incorporated the predictable general references in his brief, like other litigants, he also mentioned specific endeavors in his efforts to win out against his distinguished opponent. He gave particular emphasis to his bravery, daring, and self-sacrifice at the time of Valdivia's death. It was then that he reached the high point of his military career. As he and his witnesses told it, captain Juan Gómez was placed in command of the fort of Purén where he and a handful of men staved off hordes of Indian warriors, one of the noteworthy events in the Indies. Since Governor Valdivia had ordered him to bring reenforcements to Tucapel, captain Gómez led thirteen horsemen on the mission. They soon learned of Valdivia's capture and death, met a massive Indian attack, and saw seven of their number killed. Gómez, wounded and minus his horse that was killed in the melee, had to hide from the Indians as he made his escape. After a Spanish search party found him concealed in a field of tall grass, he helped repress the spreading rebellion and participated in the battle that proved fatal to the Araucanian commander, Lautaro.[33]

    Don Francisco was not so discourteous as to taunt Gómez about hiding from the Indians since in that instance discretion was clearly the better part of valor. Instead he concentrated on the timing of the events at Purén and Tucapel because he knew that not all the talk of those events was complimentary and some of it was particularly pejorative to Juan Gómez.

    Irarrázaval accordingly asked his witnesses if the Indians killed Pedro de Valdivia and his men because Gómez and others at Purén did not want to go to his aid and thus failed to assist him. Three depositions indicated that Valdivia had ordered Gómez to leave on a specific day before Christmas, and four faulted the horsemen for delaying their departure. Pedro de Villagra took a rather moderate stand on the consequences of the delay, remarking that if Gómez and his men had been on time, they would have proved very helpful; Governor Valdivia and some of his companions might possibly have escaped and perhaps not all the land would have been lost. As usual Juan Beltrán proffered a more emphatic, detailed opinion. If Gómez had left Purén at the appointed time, he would have arrived during the battle at Tucapel. Fourteen soldiers constituted a good relief column capable of saving Governor Valdivia and sparing Chile much of the "perdition" his death caused. In the twelve years since then, "two million" Indians--men, women and children--and over four hundred Spaniards had been killed. The war cost individuals and the king more than a million gold pesos. Furthermore, if Valdivia had lived, the royal treasury would have reaped over two million pesos.[34] Drastically inflated statistics on casualties and financial costs came quite readily to Beltrán's tongue as he contemplated the losses that resulted from "The Famous Fourteen's" tardiness.

To offset these renditions of the events of 1553 that stressed the relief column's late arrival, Gómez found it expedient to charge don Francisco with deserting Chile after spending less than a year in the war that was still in progress when he left. He called for testimony on this and wanted specific comments contrasting the duration and the quality of military services that he and don Francisco rendered. The statements forthcoming in Lima discredited don Francisco's boastful account of his war record. For instance, witnesses remembered that he had relied upon Governor Hurtado de Mendoza and Chilean residents for his support. He lacked servants, used borrowed horses, and depended on others even for his food. In the opinion of one man, he neither deserved the food he ate nor participated in any famous actions. Rodrigo de Vega Sarmiento, a Chilean treasury official, declared that don Francisco was just a boy whose quality of service differed markedly from the standard Gómez set. By now it was abundantly clear that the Chilean war was far from over when don Francisco left for Peru. While Gómez and some witnesses viewed his departure as equivalent to desertion, a few who were not overly hostile to don Francisco indicated that only part of the land was still at war when he withdrew.[35]

Don Francisco could scarcely deny that he had left Chile after only a year and fell back on the excuse that others, including high-ranking officers, left when the fighting stopped. His witness Juan Beltrán stated that Governor Hurtado de Mendoza and his men had succeeded in pacifying all the Indian rebels. Antonio Díaz Vera qualified this by asserting that the land was quieter and numerous Indians had accepted peace. Arias Pardo Maldonado said many believed that "the fury of the war" had passed. These men and others praised don Francisco's brilliant military career as a "caballero hijodalgo" who was accompanied by one or more attendants. He conducted himself like a "good soldier" and, as far as they knew, paid his own way without receiving treasury funds.[36]

As the notaries finished recording the evidence brought forward to laud or malign the respective encomienda claimants, the contradictions stood out in bold relief. From the standpoint of the crown's interest, it was fortunate that Philip II and his advisers were experienced in interpreting the hyperbole concerning personal achievements, expenses, and debts as well as the suspect data on casualties and the size and monetary worth of encomiendas.

Don Francisco and his partisans had viewed his social status in inverse proportion to the value and length of his military career; the hardships he endured were seemingly considered more severe because of the quality of his person. Juan Gómez, who questioned his opponent's fortitude and courage, ranked as an original conquistador-encomendero with almost three decades of residency in Chile and some experience in the Araucanian war, especially his leadership of "The Famous Fourteen." The pros and cons of that episode had been thoroughly aired without reaching any conclusion on what happened, and why, that would satisfy both litigants. Only the crown could decide which vassal had the better claim on the royal patrimony in the form of the Quillota encomienda.

The Chilean treasury official Rodrigo de Vega Sarmiento, an indefatigable letter writer, saw fit to advise Philip II of the financial losses the crown would sustain if either Gómez or Irarrázaval received the Quillota encomienda. Their suit, he informed the king, would arrive with his missive. He claimed that he had been physically assaulted in Lima while seeking to defend the crown's right to the Indians. Now he appealed to the king to recall that he had administered the encomienda for a year and sent the crops the villagers produced to the southern cities of Concepción and Cañete. In future, the provisions for the frontier would have to come from the royal treasury.[37]

Don Francisco also tried to weigh the scales of justice in a personal letter to Philip II. From Lima on February 1, 1566, he reminded the king of the royal decree of 1561 awarding him an encomienda and summarized the Quillota case to discredit both the treasury officials and Juan Gómez. The Indians had pertained to the crown, but the king obtained no profit from them because his treasury officials used them for personal service. Governor Villagra therefore bestowed the encomienda on don Francisco in partial fulfillment of the royal decree in his behalf. The crown attorney and Juan Gómez then brought suit to void the grant. The latter was the "most rewarded" man in Chile because he had encomiendas, including one from which he made 200,000 pesos that he "spent and gambled." He still had another that gave him an income between 3,000 and 4,000 pesos annually. "Now he comes to your royal person," don Francisco warned, "loaded with probanzas" filled with "sinister" reports to plead for "those few Indians that I have." There were approximately 200 Quillota Indians, but 600 would not suffice to fulfill the cédula of 1561. Don Francisco needed a large number of Indians because of his status as the king's servant and his great financial necessity. In a standard phrase, he stated that his only means of support derived from the king's favor. Your Majesty's servants, he admonished, have "to be preferred and especially favored and advanced in these parts where we have a greater obligation than others in the things of your royal service." He therefore petitioned for royal confirmation of the encomienda and a further reward on the basis of his standing as a royal servant, the service of his forebears, and that of his father-in-law, the House of Trade official. After this he inserted the customary mention of wife, children, and indebtedness. The king's "humble servant and vassal" owed 20,000 gold pesos that he had spent to support himself over and above his patrimony that he expended in the royal service.[38] If Philip II took the trouble to compare the figures in the letters of 1564 and 1566, he might have noticed that the debts had risen by 8,000 pesos in that short period.

Don Francisco was probably exaggerating his indebtedness, but he was correct about Juan Gómez traveling to court. While in Spain as the procurator for the city of Santiago, Gómez certified the accuracy of Ercilla's La Araucana that sang of him as the leader of "The Famous Fourteen."[39] His presence at court, and perhaps the epic verses, gave him a telling advantage over Irarrázaval. As a result, Gómez obtained a verdict awarding the Quillota encomienda to him in 1567. By that time, the decree of 1565 divesting don Francisco of the Quillota Indians and restoring them to the crown had been enforced in Chile. The ruling of 1567 meant that Philip II was giving up royal tributaries to reward Gómez. Although Gómez also won his suit for Rapel against Antonio Tarabajano, the successful encomendero died en route home from Spain and may never have known of the latter victory. His only legitimate child, don Juan de Rivadeneira, inherited the Quillota encomienda. Don Francisco de Irarrázaval, however, eventually obtained an encomienda comprised of the villages of Rapel and Pacoa.[40] Philip II honored his debts to his peninsular vassals who served him in Chile.

Chapter 3

Settling in Chile

Documentation on don Francisco de Irarrázaval's middle and later years is sparse in contrast to the lengthy encomienda litigation records.[1] Sufficient materials exist, however, to trace his steps from Peru to Chile and to observe the private and public activities that insured and reenforced the Irarrázaval y Zárate family's niche in the inner circle of the Santiago elite.

The encomienda litigation absorbed much of don Francisco's attention and accounted for some of his debts during his self-imposed exile from Chile. Among his incidental expenses were notarial fees, including a bill in October, 1566, for 138 pesos from a Lima notary for work on the Quillota case.[2] While the lawsuit helps to explain his continued presence in Peru, changes on the political scene also worked against the prompt establishment of the Irarrázaval y Zárate household in Santiago.

When don Francisco arrived in Peru in 1564, he was carrying provisional Governor Pedro de Villagra's urgent request for military assistance. He planned to return to Chile in February, 1565, with the Peruvian recruits, but the command of those forces went to a Cuzco resident, Jerónimo Costilla, who received the appointment, don Francisco informed Philip II, by virtue of his kinship with the licentiate Lope García de Castro, who headed the administration in his capacity of president of the audiencia of Lima. Acting on Castro's orders, Costilla forcibly removed Pedro de Villagra from office and installed the conquistador Rodrigo de Quiroga as interim governor. Castro had chosen Quiroga, according to don Francisco, because the men were related and both came from Galicia. Don Francisco reported on these acts of nepotism in his letter to the king on February 1, 1566, confident that Philip II would right the wrongs by providing Villagra with an appropriate reward and punishing the guilty parties. The king's servant and adviser also claimed that his role of informant constituted a special service to the crown.[3]

Philip II was not unduly concerned about the endemic partisan bickerings between the "ins" and the "outs," but he did want to improve the administrative and judicial structure as well as strengthen the military command in Chile. His answer to these problems was the creation of the audiencia of Concepción that began to function in August, 1567. Although the short-lived high court had little success in either the civil or military spheres, the audiencia ministers nevertheless proved important from the standpoint of future marital and kinship patterns. Doctor Melchor Bravo de Saravia, the president of the high court who also served as governor and captain general, and his wife doña Jerónima de Sotomayor had Chilean descendants who intermarried with Irarrázavals. So too, the granddaughter of the fiscal, the licentiate Alvar García de Navia, became the wife of an Irarrázaval. An oidor, the licentiate Juan de Torres de Vera, married into a branch of the Zárate family.[4]

Among the documents delivered to the new high court on August 12, 1567, was the royal decree of 1565 depriving don Francisco de Irarrázaval of the Quillota encomienda.[5] During his brief tenure as the absentee encomendero from 1564 to 1567, he had earned profits from approximately 250 Indians, comprising 50 work gangs, employed in gold mining.[6]

In spite of the loss of this source of income, don Francisco and doña Lorenza were at last making final preparations to move to Chile in April, 1568. At that time, he promised to pay a widow 210 pesos for a slave named Salvador and a diamond. Together he and doña Lorenza pledged surety to repay other creditors. The articles they pawned in this manner included a pearl cross, gold rosary beads set with precious stones, and ornamental buttons.[7]

After living five years in the bustling viceregal capital of Lima, setting up housekeeping in Santiago posed a challenge for doña Lorenza who had to meet responsibilities toward a growing family in a new environment. Although the tiny hamlet had been officially designated as a loyal and noble city in 1552, it boasted few amenities. The Church, it is true, provided opportunities for religious services and instructions, and some initiatives were being taken in the field of primary education for boys. Before long, young men would be able to enroll in academic courses on the secondary level as religious orders began to expand their educational offerings. Any systematic approach to educating females of course lay far in the future. The economic base of the young colony rested on placer mining and an increasing amount of rural enterprise, especially stock raising, cereal production, and viticulture. While local artisans were enlarging the scope of craft industries, commerce with Lima provided the Chilean Central Valley with a market for exports and with a supply of both utilitarian and luxury goods, including the home furnishings and the fine fabrics that colonists prized so highly. Many of the luxury items were manufactured in Europe and transshipped to South America from the isthmus of Panamá.[8]

For guidance and companionship during her early sojourn in Santiago, doña Lorenza could rely on a small group of patrician women. Missing from that group was the first and most famous Spanish woman to grace the pages of Chilean history. A few short months before doña Lorenza sailed from Peru, death claimed doña Inés Suárez whose role as a conquistadora, love affair with Pedro de Valdivia, and subsequent marriage to Rodrigo de Quiroga had won her a peerless position in conquest society.[9]

The first sizable contingents of Hispanic women had arrived in Chile in the 1550s. Outstanding among the emigrants from Spain were the widows of Governors Valdivia and Alderete, doña Marina Ortiz de Gaete and doña Esperanza de Rueda. As the heiresses to their husbands' grants of Indians, these encomenderas and erstwhile First Ladies had familiarized themselves with their new circumstances[10] while don Francisco de Irarrázaval briefly trod the military frontier, married doña Lorenza, and initiated his several appeals for rewards.

When he and doña Lorenza collected their children and belongings for the trip from Peru to Chile in 1568, another penisular, the incumbent First Lady doña Jerónima de Sotomayor, was taking similar steps. The Chileans welcomed the arrival of the <u>gobernadora</u> (governor's wife) with a bullfight. A spirit of rejoicing continued among some colonists who favored Governor Bravo, but others soon voiced their opposition to the gubernatorial family. Instead of ushering in a new era of tranquillity and justice, the tenure of the audiencia was marred with quarrels, even among its own ministers. The controversies claimed much of Governor Bravo's time while he performed his duties as chief executive and president of the high court in Concepción. The gobernadora opted to stay in Santiago with some of her children as the house guests of doña Constanza de Meneses, the daughter of one conquistador and wife of another.[11]

Although doña Lorenza and doña Jerónima were surely acquainted and perhaps became friends, they could not know that their families would eventually merge. Neither could they guess that their growing family tree would intertwine with that of the fiscal Alvar García de Navia and his wife doña Antonia de Estrada. Deep hostility between Governor Bravo and the crown attorney, who died in office,[12] probably led doña Antonia to keep her distance from the gobernadora.

In any event, the fiscal's widow had interests of her own to pursue. By 1574 she had joined the community of patrician women in Santiago where she profited from gold mining. In that year, doña Antonia registered 6,485 pesos in the treasury office, for 9 percent of the total gold submitted for the payment of the smelting fee and the royal mining tax. In 1575 she came forward with a mere 205 pesos, less than 1 percent of the total. However, by herself and as a partner of the merchant Francisco Páez de la Serna, she registered 3,607 pesos that represented 7 percent of the total in 1577. By 1592, if not before, she owned a city lot.[13]

Doña Antonia and her daughter doña Catalina Niño de Estrada obtained separate, adjoining rural land grants in 1585 from Governor Alonso de Sotomayor (probably not a relative of the former gobernadora). When doña Antonia died ten years later, doña Catalina inherited her mother's land, and Governor Alonso García Ramón validated her title to the combined acreage on September 13, 1600. As the governor noted, doña Catalina was already a widow because her husband, Pedro Olmos de Aguilera, the younger, had died "in the royal service and pacification of this kingdom" on the southern frontier. Since widowhood legally empowered her to act for herself without male supervision, doña Catalina, once her title was in order, elected to sell the land to the vecino encomendero whose Indians lived in the area. Doña Catalina had some knowledge of the legal complications that could ensue from the alienation of Indian property and the displacement of Indian residents. She therefore took care to include in the bill of sale a statement disclaiming responsibility in any suit that the Indians or the protector of the Indians might bring against the encomendero who bought the land from her. He paid the price of 140 gold pesos, not in currency but in livestock, specifically 130 choice she-goats and 100 geldings. Doña Catalina affixed her signature to the deed before a notary and three witnesses on August 24, 1604.[14]

Since doña Catalina became a trusted friend of the Irarrázaval y Zárate family, it was not surprising that friendship paved the way for a matrimonial bond between the children of these pioneering Chilean patricians. In 1620 doña Catalina's only child and heir, doña Antonia de Aguilera y Estrada, married don Fernando de Irarrázaval, the son of don Francisco and doña Lorenza.[15]

Unfortunately, no diaries or letters have been discovered to shed more direct light on the friendships and associations that doña Lorenza formed as a newcomer to Chile. Neither are inventories of household goods and personal property available to offer clues concerning the home she managed and the lifestyle she fostered. Consciously or unconsciously, however, she was a transmitter of peninsular attitudes and practices that quietly infiltrated the colony and helped to shape the way of life.

Doña Lorenza's tasks of rearing seven children and supervising the household were normal maternal responsibilities that were probably no more demanding than those of other women in her social class. There is every reason to believe that doña Lorenza, a lady of rank and station, had servants to help with the daily round of activities. She needed special initiative and fortitude, however, to direct family enterprises during those periods when her restless husband absented himself from Chile. For example, their home with its adjoining orchard and vegetable garden sustained at least minor damage when the Mapocho River flooded its banks in 1574. Doña Lorenza evidently had to cope with this crisis herself because her husband was in Charcas with her kinswoman doña Juana de Zárate and Viceroy Francisco de Toledo. It is also possible that Irarrázaval encountered doña Lorenza's brother don Fernando de Zárate, who later became the governor of Tucumán and the Río de la Plata, on this trip.[16]

The trip to Charcas served two purposes: it allowed Irarrázaval to resume his early practice of seeking out high officials and to monitor family concerns. Doña Juana, legitimated by royal decree in 1570, was the natural daughter of don Juan Ortiz de Zárate, doña Lorenza's first cousin--whose activities in Peru in the days of the Pizarros, and after, brought him wealth and prominence--and doña Leonor Yupanqui, who belonged to the Inca royal family. As her father's sole heir, doña Juana would inherit the bulk of his private estate. She was also politically important because her father had entered a special contract with the crown to govern the Río de la Plata for two lives. This meant that her future husband could act as royal governor in the vast and sparsely settled region after her father died. While her father pursued these concessions and began his official duties in modern Argentina and Paraguay, doña Juana resided in the Andean city of Chuquisaca, also known as La Plata, where Irarrázaval had the opportunity to confer with her and with Viceroy Toledo during the latter's inspection of the area. During that time, the royal decrees suppressing the audiencia of Concepción and appointing Rodrigo de Quiroga to the Chilean governorship arrived. Don Francisco was therefore a logical choice to act as courier as he wended his way home. The chronicler Alonso de Góngora Marmolejo reported on his arrival in Chile in January, 1575, with the important missives.[17]

Don Francisco had meanwhile taken up an intermittent career in local politics and thus discharged the civic duty that aristocratic status mandated. He served as a regidor (alderman) in the Santiago city council in 1571 and was elected again in 1577, but the few extant records for that year do not indicate that he ever took office. He angered the council when he declined a third term as alderman in 1584 after having served in the higher post of alcalde ordinario (magistrate and councilman) from January to April, 1581.[18] These positions on the city council were an honor and a sign of acceptance because the alcaldes and elective aldermen were chosen by the cabildo members of the previous year. In its several references to Irarrázaval, the council never failed to prefix his name with don and often referred to his status as the king's gentleman.

A further indication that don Francisco was well respected in Santiago appeared in November, 1580, and accounts for the interruption in his term as municipal magistrate in 1581. The cabildo had selected him as one of its procurators to represent the city in Lima.[19] His task as a lobbyist was to protest against two measures that threatened the Chilean encomenderos and others who engaged in mining. The first of these was the Tasa de Gamboa, a well-meaning but ineffective legislative attempt to abolish the personal service that Indians performed for their encomenderos.[20] The second was an administrative order from the Deputy Governor, doctor Luis López de Azoca, maintaining the royal mining tax at 20 percent instead of implementing a special cédula that would have reduced the rate to 10 percent.[21]

The cabildo also commissioned don Francisco as a lay representative to the Church council slated to meet in the archdiocese of Lima, but he returned to Chile before the opening sessions. He had provided an interim report on his activities in a letter received in the city council on November 21, 1581, and gave a fuller account in person on October 12, 1582. According to these documents, the question of the Tasa de Gamboa had been remitted to the Council of the Indies for a decision. The audiencia of Lima had upheld the jurisdiction of local magistrates not only in regard to court cases but also in authorizing labor contracts for nonwhites. Neither the governor nor his deputy were to intervene in these matters. The ecclesiastical tithes had also figured in don Francisco's work as a lobbyist.[22]

Regrettably, the city council minutes list only the general contents of the documents don Francisco delivered. His letter of appointment as a familiar of the Holy Office of the Inquisition appears in its entirety, however. Neither don Francisco nor his contemporaries in the cabildo manifested revulsion against that politico-ecclesiastical court. In their view it was not a reprehensible, sinister institution but merely the arm of Church and State wielding a legitimate authority in the serious matters of religious doctrine and morality. As an employee of the Inquisition, don Francisco was entitled to bear arms. His perquisites as a lay associate of the court apparently did not include a financial stipend.[23]

The mainstay of family support in any case continued to be the encomienda of Rapel and Pacoa that Irarrázaval obtained soon after settling in Chile. As time passed, first he and later doña Lorenza obtained lands in the vicinity of the latter pueblo located three leagues from Santiago. Although Spaniards alienated Indian property throughout the Indies, certain legal formalities had to be observed in order to obtain a clear title to the land. The following exposition is therefore instructive in regard to the process of building a rural estate.

On May 18, 1575, don Francisco Millapidum, the cacique of the village of Pacoa, appeared before the corregidor (district magistrate) Juan de Cuevas and identified his village as part of the Irarrázaval encomienda, to date, the first documented reference to don Francisco's having acquired possession of that grant. The cacique then petitioned for permission to sell uncultivated wastelands that he no longer needed. Cuevas appointed the protector of the Indians, Garci (sic) Suárez de Figueroa, to investigate the advisability of the sale. After conducting the on-site inspection on August 22, 1575, the protector endorsed the sale for three reasons. (1) The villagers had ample lands that were, in fact, sufficient for a larger number of Indians; (2) they would retain a large amount of very good land with first access to water from an irrigation canal (acequia); and (3) with the proceeds from the sale, they would obtain sheep that they needed to make woolen cloth to clothe themselves. The protector therefore recommended the sale of the parcel with a frontage of 178 varas.[24] According to the standard measuring device in use for land in Santiago's jurisdiction, each vara equaled 25 feet.[25] The width of the land to be sold thus measured 4,450 feet, but the length was not given.

In spite of the endorsement from the official charged with protecting Indian rights and property, nothing further was done until April 26, 1580, when the cacique don Francisco Millapidum petitioned for the sale to go forward. On the strength of the previous report from the protector, the Deputy Governor Luis López de Azoca instructed an alcalde to sell the land at auction. The deputy governor on October 20 noted an irregularity in the proceedings, however. The law required that land belonging to Indians and others with the legal status of minors had to be described by the town crier for a term of thirty days prior to accepting final bids. Since this requirement had not been met, López de Azoca ruled that the public announcements should start over and be given for thirty continuous days. These were completed by November 20, and one Andrés Ibáñez y Barroeta offered the highest bid of 202 good gold pesos, a mere 2 pesos more than another prospective buyer. The town crier called out the traditional going once, twice, and three times, and the deputy governor declared Ibáñez the new owner of the land.[26]

Two days later, Ibáñez appeared before a notary and ceded the Pacoa lands to Francisco de Lugo, who was, in fact, a middleman acting for don Francisco de Irarrázaval. As Lugo explained on February 15, 1581, don Francisco had already erected buildings and planted a vineyard on the property, invested funds in it, and now agreed to pay the 202 gold pesos for the land. Don Francisco confirmed the agreement on the same day. Although the Deputy Governor López de Azoca intervened and moved to annul the sale, the procurator and defender of the Indians, Francisco Gómez de las Montanas, entered a protest, and López de Azoca reversed himself on April 7, 1581. The deputy governor had also granted the cacique's request to have the purchase price remitted in sheep, oxen, and plowshares. To evaluate the payment in kind, Francisco Gómez and don Francisco de Irarrázaval chose two appraisers who set the price of each yoke of oxen at 18 pesos, each plowshare at 6 pesos, and each ewe at 2 *tomines* (a *tomín* equaled the eighth part of a gold peso). Don Francisco on April 8, 1581, accordingly delivered 578 mature ewes, 2 yokes of oxen, and 4 plowshares to Gómez who issued a receipt on behalf of the Indian headman.[27]

Some six years after the cacique took the first steps to exchange land for livestock and farm implements, his encomendero acquired title to the property. Why the deputy governor had sought to nullify the auction is not explained in the documentation. Perhaps he was making an honest effort to defend the rights of the Indian proprietors. López de Azoca, however, was known as a greedy man[28] and may have delayed the sale in order to induce Irarrázaval to offer him some form of gratuity. If such bargaining did take place, don Francisco had a trump card because he was on the verge of leaving for Peru to undertake his lobbying duties on behalf of the city of Santiago.[29] Reporting on López de Azoca was part of his formal charge from the cabildo which could conceivably be expanded to include further allegations against the deputy governor. In any event, the cacique don Francisco Millapidum had lent himself to a legal business transaction that he apparently viewed as profitable for himself and his people.

Irarrázaval, on the other hand, had capitalized on the encomienda villagers' need for livestock and implements of European origin to become a rural landowner. Since ownership of an estancia or hacienda was a widespread elite aspiration and fast becoming mandatory for full membership in the topmost level of society, he had met an important goal through the outlay of a modest sum of money. From the financial standpoint, the family fortune would grow as land appreciated in value. The administration of the new royally-appointed Governor, don Alonso de Sotomayor, would hold additional advantages for don Francisco, his wife, and their descendants.

Shortly after don Francisco returned from Lima, Sotomayor marched into Chile across the Andean route in 1583 at the head of several hundred Europeans destined for service on the southern military frontier. Although he was only approximately thirty years old, he had participated in European campaigns and obtained membership in the Order of Santiago.[30] In Chile, Sotomayor compiled a mixed, but primarily negative, record in regard to Indian labor legislation because he revoked the beneficial provisions of the Tasa de Gamboa yet made administrative appointments to curb some of the more excessive forms of exploitation. The encomendero class welcomed his abolition of the monetary tribute established in the Tasa de Gamboa and the official restoration of Indian personal service.[31]

As a member of the elite corps, Irarrázaval now had the opportunity to put the Pacoa tributaries to work on his land adjacent to their village, and he soon had a further reason for becoming a gubernatorial partisan. On September 22, 1584, Governor Sotomayor awarded don Francisco a land grant on the Pacific coast that added to the acreage under the Irarrázaval y Zárate family's control.[32]

Another sign of financial resources and affluence that undermines don Francisco's self-proclaimed poverty, concerned his ownership of Negroid slaves. For example, on July 28, 1585, the child Juan, the legitimate son of Catalina, an Indian, and her husband, don Francisco's black slave Ponce, was baptized in the Santiago cathedral.[33]

In spite of his wealth and standing, the trail through the last years of don Francisco's life grows so dim that even the date and place of his death are unclear. It is probable that he died in Chuquisaca late in 1589 when he was visiting doña Lorenza's brother don Fernando.[34] In any case, he had resided in Chile for approximately twenty years and with his wife advanced the family interests.

The couple's oldest surviving son, don Francisco's namesake, eventually moved to Spain and claimed the Irarrázaval inheritance that devolved upon him because his father's older brother died without heirs. As a youth, young don Francisco had gravitated toward Chuquisaca, perhaps as his father's companion on that last journey. Although doña Juana de Zárate had died in 1584, her widower, the licentiate Juan de Torres de Vera, the former oidor in the high court of Concepción, was living there. They had been married after his transfer to the audiencia of Charcas, and he finally became governor of the Río de la Plata. In Madrid in 1594, Torres de Vera testified to young Irarrázaval's services in South America. Don Francisco de Irarrázaval y Zárate soon went on to command military forces in Philip III's European campaigns, hold royal appointments, join the Order of Santiago, and garner hereditary titles of nobility as a <u>vizconde</u> and a <u>marqués</u>. He married twice, each time a woman of distinction. His sister doña Leonor de Recalde also settled in Spain and entered two prestigious marriages.[35]

Doña Leonor tried to persuade their sister doña Angela de Zárate, who became a nun and later the abbess of a Lima nunnery, to transfer to a convent in Spain, but the latter preferred to stay in Lima. Meanwhile, their brother don Diego de Zárate attached himself to their maternal uncle, don Fernando de Zárate, and established himself in Chuquisaca. The baptismal records for doña Angela and don Diego, dating from 1581 and 1583, have withstood the tests of time, humidity, and defective pens rather well in the ecclesiastical archives in Santiago. (Abstracts of parish records appear in Appendix 1.) Doña Angela's godfather was a member of the proud Quiroga family. Don Diego's godparents were Alonso Campofrío de Carvajal, who came to Chile in the Hurtado de Mendoza expedition with don Francisco de Irarrázaval and the poet Ercilla, and doña Mariana de Riberos, his creole wife. Doña Mariana was the daughter of a conquistador and the grandniece of doña Marina Ortiz de Gaete, the wife of Pedro de Valdivia.[36] The circle of friendship and affinity within which the Irarrázaval y Zárate family moved thus included old line patricians.

Although her children were scattering far from Chile, doña Lorenza de Zárate had reasons for staying in her adopted homeland during the Sotomayor administration. She now had to assume responsibility for guiding the family destiny and began to exercise the independence that Spanish law conferred on widows. Through advice and counsel, she undoubtedly influenced family decisions during her husband's lifetime but, in public acts and legal transactions, she had maintained a low profile. Doña Lorenza, as we have seen, had occasion to gain experience in coping with problems when don Francisco was away from Chile. These lessons in self-reliance, whether welcome or not, fortified her for widowhood. When he died, she was at least somewhat prepared for her new role and became more active and visible in steering a course for herself and the young children still at home. Friends, especially her children's godparents, bound to her as *compadres* through the relationship known as *compadrazgo*, could of course be counted on for assistance.

During those early years of her widowhood, doña Lorenza also benefited from Governor Sotomayor's attentive concern. He was paying court to her daughter doña Isabel de Zárate, and it is probable that marital negotiations were in progress before don Francisco died. Be that as it may, the young couple were secretly married on January 12, 1590. The witnesses were the bridegroom's trusted friend from the time they met in Spain and traveled to Chile together, don Ramiriáñez Bravo de Saravia, and his wife doña Isabel Osorio de Cáceres. Their parentage attests to the patrician status of the witnesses: Bravo was the son of the former governor, and doña Isabel was the daughter of a conquistador and his peninsular wife. An Indian village in the Bravo encomienda was the setting for the exchange of vows and the nuptial blessing (velación). The witnesses and the locale prefigured, in a sense, the latter-day union of the Chilean branches of the Bravo de Saravia and Irarrázaval families.[37]

Since the bride's family was no doubt still in mourning for her father, a quiet wedding was appropriate. There was, however, a weightier reason for the lack of fanfare. From the earliest days of the conquest of the Indies, a hue and cry had gone up against nepotism and other forms of official favoritism. As time passed, the clamor increased because of the propensity of royal administrators and judges to marry local women while in office or to arrange marriages for their offspring or relatives. The chief sounding board for these complaints was the crown, and in 1575 Philip II responded with a law designed to insure a more impartial exercise of judicial authority by prohibiting the marriages not only of viceroys and audiencia ministers but also of their children within their jurisdictional districts. A special royal license to marry could be obtained, however, and this loophole, along with the penalty of loss of office, reappeared in the decree of 1582 that extended the ban to governors and other royally appointed administrators but not their children. As recent studies have shown, these laws were never fully effective nor uniformly enforced.[38]

One of the first oidores caught by the new legislation was Juan de Torres de Vera, the oidor of Charcas, whose clandestine marriage to doña Juana de

Zárate and efforts to obtain the Platine governorship occurred against a background of political opposition and intrigue that set off protracted lawsuits. The example of their difficulties and his ultimate victory in winning the coveted post from the crown in 1583[39] could scarcely be discounted by doña Juana's Chilean relatives when they contemplated the Sotomayor-Zárate union.

Chilean historians disagree about the effect of Governor Sotomayor's marriage on his official career, with one surmising that he obtained the necessary royal permission to marry, and another stating that the illegal marriage prompted the king to replace him.[40] In either case, don Alonso was already the object, like other political figures then and now, of sharp criticism and the infraction added fuel to the fire when it became known. Although he continued to have backers, critics who insisted that he had spent too much time enjoying himself in Santiago instead of campaigning in the south could remark that the new bridegroom was even more reluctant to go to the frontier. Among the first to inform the king that the marriage distracted don Alonso from his military duties as captain general was don García Hurtado de Mendoza, the ex-governor of Chile and now viceroy of Peru.[41]

The marriage did not, however, plunge Sotomayor into permanent disgrace and oblivion. Hurtado de Mendoza posted him to Central America in 1595, and he became governor, captain general, and president of the audiencia of Panamá by royal appointment the following year. When he retired to Spain in 1604, he declined an offer for a second term in Chile but soon accepted a seat on the royal Council of War and thereby became an ex officio member of the Junta de Guerra that advised the king on military matters concerning the Indies.[42] A final sign of royal approval of don Alonso and his chosen wife was the noble title of marquesa that Philip IV granted to their daughter doña Lorenza de Sotomayor y Zárate.[43]

As soon as it occurred, the marriage provided advantages for the Irarrázaval y Zárate family. It not only verified high social standing but also brought tangible rewards. The most obvious of these was the land grant don Alonso bestowed on his mother-in-law. Six months after the wedding, on July 26, 1590, in Santiago, he issued her a land title to acreage in the Pacoa district where her husband had earlier purchased land from his encomienda Indians. The deed carried the proviso, found in others that Sotomayor granted, that doña Lorenza de Zárate had to obtain royal confirmation within three years.[44] She did not take formal possession, however, until March 21, 1594, after her son-in-law's administration had ended. There was no mention of royal confirmation at this time or in 1602 when Governor Alonso de Ribera confirmed the title for her heirs. During a general land survey of the Santiago region in 1604, a cacique, three Indian men, and one Indian widow still retained a small amount of private and communal property in the locality. The rest of the Pacoa lands comprised the estancia that doña Lorenza and her husband had acquired.[45]

When doña Lorenza managed the estancia during her widowhood, it produced livestock, grain, flax, and wine. An inventory dating from the early 1590s states that, in addition to a vineyard, there were cultivated fields, houses, a warehouse and vessels for storing wine, and a storeroom stocked with maize and wheat. Also on hand were flax ready to be dressed, lime for the vineyard, carts, and assorted tools. The livestock included oxen, goats, and swine as well as cattle and sheep. Doña Lorenza had fourteen Indians subject to her orders working on the estancia along with twenty-six others from an encomienda that Governor Sotomayor had appropriated for himself. Since he acquired more than one encomienda during his governorship but had to attend to affairs of state and military matters, his wife doña Isabel signed receipts for tribute that some Indians rendered him in gold.[46] The governor, the First Lady, and her mother thus all profited from Indian labor.

The gobernadora had the authority to receive Indian tribute in her husband's name because he had issued her a power of attorney on November 4, 1590, appointing her his proxy in legal and business matters. It was copied verbatim when doña Isabel sold two farms (chácaras) near Santiago that he had obtained before their marriage. The purchaser, Jerónimo de Molina, on April 3, 1591, received a deed to the land itself, half of the maize planted on it, the buildings, and a vineyard. The bill of sale, which doña Isabel de Zárate signed, also enumerated the following items: 10 yokes of oxen, 8 carts, carpentry tools, plows, hoes, mattocks, and sickles.

All the earthern jars used for storing wine were included except 10 new ones that belonged to her mother doña Lorenza. The selling price was 5,900 gold pesos; doña Isabel accepted 2,900 in cash, and the purchaser assumed responsibility for censos (interest-bearing cash loans guaranteed with real estate) worth 3,000 pesos. The creditors holding the liens on the farms were 19 Indian pueblos. The money had come from their communal assets (cajas de las comunidades). It had been loaned, in amounts ranging from a low of 33 pesos to a high of 584 pesos, at the then prevailing rate of 5 percent simple interest. As stated in the bill of sale, Molina's immediate obligation was to meet the annual interest payments of some 200 pesos. He repaid the principal within four years, however.[47]

It was commonplace for Spaniards to encumber their property with censos, but this type of mortgage rather than impeding the transfer of real estate actually facilitated it because purchasers did not have to make large outlays of cash.[48] In this instance, doña Isabel, in her husband's name, had not only paid debts owed to Indian villages but obtained liquid assets. They would need the money because he had already been in office for eight years and, whether the crown smiled or frowned on their marriage, it was only a matter of time until a new governor would replace him.

The Sotomayor administration was a bittersweet phase in the life of doña Lorenza de Zárate, the First Lady's mother. Her daughter's marriage was, on the one hand, a source of pride and helped the family flourish and, on the other, a factor coalescing the factions for and against the governor that were so typical of colonial politics. Fortunately, doña Lorenza's experiences both as the daughter of a crown official in Seville and as the wife of a man wise in the ways of court, viceregal, and gubernatorial maneuvering prepared her to cope with the praise and blame heaped on her son-in-law. Nothing could shield her, however, from personal grief and anxiety. She learned of her husband's death while their eldest son don Carlos was an officer in the Araucanian war. Don Carlos, who owed his commissions to Governor Sotomayor, died, not in combat but of accidental drowning, in 1592.[49]

Doña Lorenza thus had to put aside her sense of loss and look to the future as the head of her family. She accordingly appeared in local magistracy court to obtain the legal guardianship of her young son don Fernando on May 4, 1593. Doña Lorenza presented her petition to the licentiate Juan de Morales Negrete, the alcalde who conducted the hearing, before the notary Ginés de Toro Mazote. She personally swore the solemn oath required of tutors and guardians and with her bondsman Gaspar Jorge de Segura pledged financial surety for the faithful performance of her duties. With the legal forms in order, the alcalde, doña Lorenza, Gaspar, the official witnesses, and the notary affixed their signatures to the document.[50]

This action illustrates that doña Lorenza, like her fellow colonists throughout the Indies, adhered to the Castilian precepts that prevailed in the realm of private law, including the trusteeship of minors. With its well-known provisions regarding community property, legislation handed down from medieval Castile became an enduring feature of the Spanish presence in America. While the Castilian laws of inheritance allowed mothers and fathers to make special, limited bequests to one or more heirs in the direct line, parents could not violate the basic legal principle that designated all legitimate children, male and female, as co-heirs to the paternal and maternal estates. The law also defined a daughter's marital dowry (<u>dote</u>) and a son's gifts by reason of marriage (<u>donacionces</u> <u>propter</u> <u>nupcias</u>) as shares of the inheritance to be counted in the final division of the parental assets.[51]

As a widow, doña Lorenza demonstrated her familiarity with the laws of inheritance and with that curious yet legal prerogative of empowering proxies to draft a posthumous will. The latter proved useful to many colonists who lacked the time or inclination to make their wills in person. Doña Lorenza first prepared an informal memorandum outlining her wishes. Then on July 13, 1593, she issued a notarized power of attorney to her daughter doña Isabel de Zárate and son-in-law don Alonso de Sotomayor to compose her posthumous will and act as executors of the estate. She designated her legitimate children as heirs, with the exception of her daughters doña Isabel and doña Leonor who had already received their inheritance in the form of dowries. Doña Lorenza de Zárate signed her name to the power of attorney in Santiago before the notary Ginés de Toro Mazote and three male witnesses.[52]

The document was both legal and thoroughly typical of the testamentary dispositions of mothers and fathers who followed the legislative mandates calling for a fair and equitable division of their assets. It indicates that doña Lorenza, as she neared the end of her life, was a prudent woman. She used a device, sanctioned by law, that would serve as a precaution against dying intestate and burdening the children with settling her affairs. The power of attorney also obviated the problems that could arise from writing a will too early. Colonists who did this often had to encumber the original will with codicils to take changed circumstances into account.

Doña Lorenza named her proxies and gave them her power of attorney when she was planning to leave Chile and feared an untimely death on the journey. She had already settled the troublesome question of the Irarrázaval encomienda title. According to the then current law and practice of holding an encomienda for two lives, her son don Carlos had inherited the title from his father, and the Indians had escheated to the crown when the heir died. To forestall the loss of the Indians, doña Lorenza petitioned Governor Martín García Oñez de Loyola for her young son don Fernando to become the encomendero. The governor denied her request because this would constitute a "third life" but appointed her the administrator of the Indians in return for a loan to the treasury of 1,000 gold pesos. Dissatisfied with this compromise, she appealed to Viceroy Hurtado de Mendoza, who in March, 1593, granted the encomienda to the boy. According to the terms of the viceregal ruling, the monetary loan would become an outright gift to the crown. During her last years in Chile, doña Lorenza managed the encomienda[53] and, as we have seen, used some of the Indians as workers on the Pacoa estancia.

As the payment to the treasury indicates, the widowed mother sometimes needed ready cash, and doña Lorenza on three occasions borrowed money in the form of censos from pueblo funds disbursed by the protector of the Indians. A document dating from 1594 shows that she and her children owed Indian communities a total of 2,319 pesos and 5 tomines. One of the villages, Rapel, pertained to the Irarrázaval encomienda.[54]

Although the document fails to state which real estate she pledged as collateral for the loans, the rural lands already obtained through purchase and gubernatorial grants were available for this purpose. In addition, doña Lorenza held title to two city lots. One was sold in 1596, but the other remained in her name in 1599.[55]

By that time, doña Lorenza was far from Chile, never to return. She and don Fernando had accompanied or followed her daughter and son-in-law to Sotomayor's new assignment in Panamá. Viceroy Hurtado de Mendoza commissioned Sotomayor for that tour of duty with orders to repel English pirates. Although Sir Francis Drake attacked the Caribbean coast between December, 1595, and January, 1596, neither his health nor his forces were strong enough to cross the isthmus and take the city of Panamá.[56] The residents nevertheless feared that he would succeed while Sotomayor was absent from the city, and the episode provided material for an eyewitness narrative by don Alonso's friend and biographer, Francisco Caro de Torres.

As he told it, doña Lorenza de Zárate inspired the Panamanians to resist the foreign enemies. Standing on a chair in the plaza, the "brave lady...with masculine vigor" urged them to fight fearlessly to the death and promised to help defend the city. She assured them she had shown her spirit in Chile "where she had lived more than thirty years and seen many tumults of war." She identified her late husband as a royal page and gentleman of the king's household who had served in Chile under Hurtado de Mendoza and subsequent governors and become a resident of Santiago where their daughter married don Alonso de Sotomayor.[57]

The small book incorporating this aside belongs to that genre of historical writing designed to laud illustrious persons and families and ultimately help them secure or maintain royal recognition. In this case, the chronicler wrote on behalf of don Carlos de Sotomayor y Zárate, the grandson of doña Lorenza and don Francisco.[58] As a result, it is impossible to determine whether she made any such brave speech. If she did so, she may have been inspired by stories of other women who had proved their valor in Chile. On the other hand, her admirer may have fabricated his rendition from the myths and realities that were recounted about Chilean warrior women who, unlike doña Lorenza, lived in the southern war zone.

While Caro de Torres was not above the use of literary license that, of itself, provides an insight into the aristocratic mentality, his chronicle also reproduces documentary evidence. For example, he incorporated the formal endorsement from the high court of Panamá for don Alonso de Sotomayor as a candidate for royal favors. The audiencia ministers who praised Sotomayor for his help against Drake mentioned that his wife was doña Isabel de Zárate, a "renowned woman." However, the judges did not attribute any role to her mother in rallying resistance to the English.[59] The omission does little to resolve the question of how doña Lorenza conducted herself in Panamá. Other records indicate that she died there in 1601.[60]

Don Francisco de Irarrázaval and doña Lorenza de Zárate had lived eventful lives in the early formative period following the initial phase of the Chilean conquest. Set apart from commoners by reason of their lineage and upbringing, they did much to transplant peninsular aristocratic attitudes and values to the new land and to instill them in their children.

Only their son don Fernando returned to Santiago to preserve the family presence in the southern realm. After he left Chile with his mother, he was away until 1620. During that time, he gave doña Catalina Niño de Estrada a power of attorney to handle his Chilean property. When he relinquished his encomienda, she obtained title to it. Her daughter doña Antonia de Aguilera y Estrada inherited it, married don Fernando upon his return to Chile, and brought him a dowry in excess of 30,000 pesos that included land in the district of Rapel.[61] The marriage not only restored don Fernando to the ranks of the Chilean vecinos feudatarios but also endowed the Irarrázavals of the next generation with a proud maternal lineage.

Seniority in the conquest had always carried weight. The Aguileras were related to Pedro de Valdivia, and doña Antonia's paternal grandfather, Pedro Olmos de Aguilera, participated in the conquest with him in the 1550s. The creole bride therefore formed a significant link in the ancestral chain leading back to Valdivia's day that had been missing from the Irarrázaval y Zárate family tree. Her maternal grandfather, the licentiate Alvar Garcia de Navia, was a most cantankerous high court minister during his tenure as the fiscal of the audiencia of Concepción. Once he was safely entombed, however, his widow and descendants had strong leverage in pleading for royal favors to compensate for his service in what was an admittedly important post.[62] As previously indicated, doña Antonia's father Pedro Olmos de Aguilera, the younger, died on the southern frontier. This marked him as a vassal who had made the ultimate sacrifice for his king.

The legacy of not only merits and services but also material affluence that don Fernando and doña Antonia received was passed on to their distinguished descendants in both Chile and Spain.[63] Colonists who lacked elite credentials were meanwhile emulating the aristocracy and seeking to join it.

PART II

SOCIAL CLIMBERS

As the social hierarchy evolved during the Hapsburg era, the aristocracy maintained a jealously-guarded hold over its position in Chilean society but, on occasion, did admit the exceptional and successful outsider deemed worthy to marry into the entrenched families.[1] Since the upper social scale was divided into components, its internal structure requires further attention before considering social climbers whose income bracket, occupation, and personal attributes made it possible for them to improve their standing.[2]

The inner circle of patricians at the top of the social ladder consisted of the foremost families claiming hidalguía, although genteel status was sometimes exaggerated, if not entirely fabricated, and a long hereditary record of service to the crown since the opening phase of the conquest. These "first families" were householders and landowners who boasted encomiendas, comprising one or more pueblos that still retained at least a nominal village identity even if the Indians themselves had been settled on the encomendero's property. The vecinos feudatarios held their grants as visible recognition of cumulative merits and services. To further enhance their prestige, the Irarrázavals and several other patrician families established marital and kinship networks with colonial officialdom.

Beneath the patriciate stood landowning families who fell just short of the qualifications of their social superiors. This group included less distinguished branches of a notable family as well as newcomers and therefore found it more difficult to prove gentility. The encomenderos on this level--and command of some form of servile labor was a must--held newly formed grants of tributaries who had lost contact with any native village or headman. The Indians had previously been yanaconas, slaves brought from the Araucanian country, or natives of the province of Cuyo. In some cases, large encomiendas were divided in order to assign tributaries to a new encomendero.

Undulating lines separated the merely prominent lower level aristocrats from those directly above and immediately below them in society. Since individuals were rated on both a personal and class basis, it is sometimes impossible to learn why one person won acceptance and another did not. The subjective element was nonetheless present as the aristocracy, divided as it was, and the middle groups interacted with each other. As a result of this rather nebulous process, the upper classes in Santiago gradually increased in size. The patricians admitted members of the newer elite into the fold, and individuals and families from the intermediate ranges of society gained positions in the lower level aristocracy.

Chileans employed a rich vocabulary to describe the degrees of difference between and within the upper and middle social strata. The terms themselves underwent change and new connotations crept in to accommodate the changes in the fabric of society. In line with sixteenth-century Peruvian practice, the use of doña became so widespread that it applied to almost any woman above frankly plebian status.[3] The masculine equivalent, don, gradually began to lose its aristocratic exclusiveness in the seventeenth century. As we have already seen, the courtly medieval phrase, caballero hijodalgo, became less restricted as commoners appropriated it to themselves. Fortunately, documentary materials contain further clues for solving the word puzzle that in turn sheds light on the social structure.

The original conquistadores-encomenderos had explained and defended their self-evident predominance when they documented their merits and services. Their descendants and heirs to their encomiendas kept alive the conjunction between conquest and colonization by referring to themselves as the children and grandchildren of the first conquerors and settlers of the new land. These persons, as already mentioned, held the rank of patricians as feudatarios. They often used the synonym <u>vecinos encomenderos</u>, or the shortened form vecinos, to indicate their exalted status.[4]

In Castile, however, a vecino was merely a

permanent, established resident in a city or town, and the crown applied the Castilian meaning in its sixteenth-century rulings on eligibility for cabildo membership. A special cédula directed to Chile in 1554 stated that only vecinos could be elected as alcaldes and regidores and defined a vecino as a resident male householder in a city, one who had a substantial household, a "casa poblada," regardless of whether he had an encomienda.[5]

Although the decree did not open the door to all commoners, the encomenderos continued to regard themselves as the only genuine vecinos. More significantly, they monopolized the Santiago council until a group of non-encomenderos challenged them in the 1570s. The leader of the disenfranchised residents, Jerónimo de Molina, obtained an injunction and covering letter from the audiencia of Concepción in 1575 ordering that henceforth one-half of the elective positions (alcaldías and regimientos) should be filled with vecinos encomenderos and one-half should go to the other "vecinos and moradores of that city who have a house and residency, although they do not have encomienda Indians." To win the case, Molina, a landowning merchant who later purchased the Sotomayor farm, had cited the names and stature of individuals who had previously been excluded, calling particular attention to the licentiate Juan Francisco de Escobedo and to merchants like himself who met the definition of vecino given in the decree of 1554. He referred to these men by the several terms denoting residency: "vecinos and moradores and ciudadanos."[6]

The city council reluctantly complied with the

court order that was upheld by the audiencia of Lima. Beginning in 1577, one alcalde was a vecino encomendero and the other was a vecino morador; the six elective regimientos were also divided between the two social groups.[7] The principle continued to be applied, but with considerable rule-bending, in the seventeenth century. Some vecinos encomenderos were elected to the regimientos designated for vecinos moradores, and the alcalde's staff of office reserved for a vecino encomendero sometimes went to a vecino morador. These elections indicate that a good deal of slipping and sliding was taking place on the social ladder.[8] In the balloting process, the electors were using subjective criteria and failing to hold the line between vecinos and moradores.

Throughout the seventeenth century, the city councilmen identified themselves as His Majesty's loyal vassals, serving now in the council chamber far from the southern battlefields. While they stretched the concept of vassalage beyond its original medieval meaning that presupposed noble status, they stripped the sixteenth-century form of address, "very magnificient señores" (lords and gentlemen), of its pompous modifiers. Occasionally, however, the cabildo records reaffirm the contrast within the encomendero class between the old, established elite and the lesser yet still prominent individuals. The best examples are those occasions when the city council formally recognized one of the latter who was registering his new status as a feudatario. The final step into the inner circle of patricians merited a small ceremony. As these same documents attest, a vecino feudatario was entitled to certain honors and perquisites. For tax purposes and in meetings devoted to economic policies, the cabildo found the term cosecheros (producers) useful to encompass landowners, with and without encomiendas, who were socially superior to merchants (mercaderes, comerciantes).[9]

During the Hapsburg era, the middle groups in society included not only the commercial element but also officers in the frontier army, bureaucrats, and professional men such as lawyers and notaries. The wives, daughters, and sisters of these men shared their social status and were often instrumental in improving family prospects.[10]

There were no hard and fast rules governing social mobility as people moved up and down the social ladder and across the barricades that separated classes and groups. Men and women moving at their own rate of speed upset any sociological patterns that might seem to be emerging. As they exerted their individual initiative and responded to their personal motivations, existing conditions and situations could either help or hinder their progress. With these cautions in mind, it is possible to sketch some generalizations that, in spite of particular cases that disproved the rule, usually held true.

Wealth by itself could not buy entry into the upper classes. Money was necessary for upward mobility, but even with a massive fortune it was rare, if not unheard of, for "a nobody" to skip the intervening rungs on the social ladder and reach the higher levels. A prospector might literally strike gold and yet remain in the same niche in society. If newly earned or discovered riches were used to effect a more genteel lifestyle and occupation, however, they accelerated the process of advancement. Still, in the normal course of events, the process was slow, and upward mobility required not one lifetime but two or more generations.

A quantitative correlation between affluence and social status during the colonial period has not been, and may never be, established. Through wise investments, some commercial families nevertheless made not only financial but social gains. For example, a rich merchant might marry a woman who outranked him but lacked a marriage portion sufficient to attract a more prominent suitor. Newcomers, most often from Spain or neighboring Peru, who were commissioned as officers in the frontier army found that their military titles, even those bestowed on officers in local militia units, carried weight with Chileans. Education could also win respect if the youth achieved the licentiate degree, usually in law. Acquiring a government office was itself a sign of having achieved some stature and could become a springboard for higher things. A number of bureaucratic positions were always filled through gubernatorial patronage. Beginning in the late sixteenth and early seventeenth centuries, qualified candidates could purchase certain public offices from the crown. When the owners gained the right to transfer these vendible offices, upon the payment of a hefty tax to the royal treasury, both political and social consequences ensued.[11] (Appendix 2 lists royal revenue derived from offices mentioned in the text.)

The several avenues to social advancement are examined in more detail in the following chapters concerning the Toro Mazote clan. The family, including its forebears and descendants, furnishes examples of up-and-coming social climbers in the sixteenth and seventeenth centuries.

Chapter 4

Obscure Family Origins

The maternal line of the Toro Mazote family originated in Chile with Andrés Hernández, a peninsular, and his wife Magdalena de la Serna, whose background contained those blind spots that plague genealogists. They are unsure, for example, of her parentage and unable to establish where and when she married Andrés. It would seem that Magdalena's father was probably Agustín de la Serna, an encomendero and city councilman in La Serena who was killed when Indians destroyed the small town in 1549. Perhaps her mother was an Indian woman.[1] If so, Magdalena's status as a mestiza constituted a racial obstacle for her descendants to overcome. This could account for the apparent absence of documentation on merits and services because her descendants would have ferreted out proofs of distinguished ancestors had they existed. Since a veil of obscurity covers Magdalena's origins, the evidence remains conjectural and therefore suggests that she lacked an illustrious lineage.

Sixteenth-century treasury records furnish information on Andrés Hernández, who became a wealthy merchant in Santiago. During the gold mining era, a merchant's customers often paid for goods with unsmelted gold. He then took the gold to the treasury office to pay the smelting fee and the royal mining tax. This practice evidently accounts for the 62,687 gold pesos Andrés registered in the treasury office between 1567-1569 and 1573-1577. In that same period, he and several associates jointly registered an additional 6,280 pesos for a total of 68,967 pesos.[2] After allowances are made for overhead expenses and the cost of importing merchandise from Peru, this still represented a sizable income.

Hernández became the tithe farmer in the diocese of Santiago in 1573, a position that entitled him to collect the tax on rural commodities used to support the Church. The contract he negotiated required him to remit 3,800 gold pesos. If he failed to collect that sum, he would have to pay the difference himself; should he collect more, the profit was his to keep.[3]

Since tithe farming involved an element of speculation, Hernández prudently looked to more stable forms of investment. Examples are found in his real estate transactions. Andrés owned seven pieces of urban property, six lots and a vineyard, shown on the city plat. One city lot was probably the site of his shop and the Hernández de la Serna home, but others may have been rented out. In 1581 he obtained a rural estancia in a gubernatorial grant. Although the estancia and three city lots were handed down to Hernández de la Serna children, other lots and the vineyard were sold soon after they were acquired,[4] no doubt with an eye for profit.

Becoming a landowner and resident householder (vecino morador) was a small but definite step up the social ladder that qualified Hernández for cabildo membership, and he served one term as an elected alderman in 1590.[5] Notwithstanding their affluence and improved stature, Andrés Hernández and Magdalena de la Serna never belonged to the upper class. Something was missing--something that money and property could not buy--and whatever it was prevented their children from marrying into the patriciate.

For example, their sons Melchor and Andrés Hernández de la Serna married women with the proud name of Cáceres, but their mother was the natural daughter of a conquistador and probably a mestiza. Although illegitimacy and racial mixture were not insurmountable social obstacles, they were impediments difficult to overcome. As a result, the Cáceres sisters could hardly compete with their relative doña Isabel Osorio de Cáceres, poised comfortably within the patrician elite. Nor did Andrés Hernández de la Serna's second marriage notably improve his standing because his second wife was similar in lineage and rank to the first. Intangible yet real restraints also retarded the social mobility of the other Hernández de la Serna children who married. Their spouses came from the middle rather than the upper levels of society. The case that is pertinent here concerns Ginés de Toro Mazote, the husband of doña Elena de la Serna.[6]

Doña Elena's father was already making a name for

himself as a merchant when Ginés de Toro Mazote, a native son of Madrid, was beginning his life in Chile. It is possible that the young peninsular was related to the conquistador-encomendero Francisco Martínez, who invested heavily in the Valdivia expedition.[7] Such a kinship tie would help explain why Ginés chose to settle in Chile, but the relationship cannot be verified. Firmer evidence exists concerning his arrival as a soldier with a military contingent about 1567 and his tour of duty on the Araucanian frontier. After being wounded in the arm, he went to live in Santiago.[8]

By 1575 Toro Mazote had become a merchant and in that year took 1,084 gold pesos to the treasury office; he registered 2,038 pesos in 1576.[9] As a man with a head for business, he was welcome in the Hernández de la Serna household, and he and doña Elena de la Serna were husband and wife by 1577. Doña Elena received a marriage portion worth 8,000 pesos and, while still a very young matron, an additional maternal inheritance of 1,000 pesos.[10]

Doña Elena's dowry-inheritance is indicative of her parents' wealth because parental estates were divisible among all the heirs,[11] and she had no fewer than six brothers and sisters. Her 9,000 pesos were also an important financial base for the newlyweds.

Ginés was not a model husband in terms of marital fidelity, however. In 1581 his mestizo son by the Indian woman María was baptized in the Santiago cathedral. Some ten years later, he formed a liaison with the Indian Juliana and recognized their son Juan at his baptism. The historian Tomás Thayer Ojeda mentions an illegitimate daughter. Ginés and doña Elena had thirteen legitimate children who survived their father.[12]

With these numerous paternal responsibilities, Ginés needed steady employment, and a satisfactory career opportunity presented itself in 1584. Alonso de Zapata, who owned the dual office of notary public and cabildo clerk, was ready to step down and willing to transfer it through the renunciation process. This procedure, established by recent legislation, required a prospective notary to pay a fraction of the office's assessed value to the crown. The bargain that Toro Mazote struck with Zapata priced the notarial office at 3,500 gold pesos. Governor Sotomayor, who was supervising the transfer, required Toro Mazote to remit one-third of that sum to the treasury and issued him a title to the office. All vendible posts required royal confirmation, and this the new notary obtained, not without delays, in 1590. He had undertaken his duties in January, 1585, and worked as the cabildo clerk and a notary until he renounced the combined positions in favor of his son Manuel in August, 1606, shortly before he died.[13]

Ginés de Toro Mazote was availing himself of several paths to social and economic advancement. As the law allowed, he had become the administrator of his wife's substantial marital endowment and inheritance. While continuing to engage in trade as a merchant, he entered the lower echelons of the professional class when he became a proprietary notary.[14] In that capacity, he had inside information on every type of official and private business taking place in the capital city. He knew the contents of royal decrees, executive orders from viceroys and governors, and impending city ordinances before they became public knowledge, and heard the councilmen discuss these matters in their secret sessions. As the notary of record for clients registering everything from marital contracts, bills of sale, business partnerships, powers of attorney, and loans to last wills and testaments, he had a finger on the pulse of the city.[15]

Despite its advantages, Toro Mazote's position in the bureaucracy had its financial drawbacks. In the first place, he had spent a great deal of money in acquiring the office. Secondly, the fees he collected for notarizing individual documents were low. Thirdly, the annual salary due the cabildo clerk was only 200 pesos and sometimes in arrears. He turned this to good account, however, by convincing the council to grant him city lots in lieu of monetary payments in 1586.[16]

Over the years, Ginés and his wife doña Elena de la Serna acquired additional urban property.[17] He also launched an ambitious and rather deliberate campaign to become a rural landowner. By 1591 he had purchased a farm belonging to doña Magdalena de Miranda. When the posthumous estate of one Cristóbal Hernández (probably doña Elena's brother) was being settled, Ginés bought his large chácara that included a vineyard. In a series of transactions, Ginés consolidated other farms into an estancia. One of the deeds was questionable until Governor Alonso de Ribera confirmed it for him in 1602, with appropriate acknowledgements of his service to the crown as a notary, permanent residency in Chile, and responsibility as husband, father, and head of a large household. The gubernatorial confirmation was a wise precaution because land titles were inspected during the general land survey that was getting under way within Santiago's jurisdiction. The notary who recorded documents during the survey was doña Elena's brother, Melchor Hernández de la Serna. Two men who were affiliated with her family through marriage had owned farms that her husband incorporated in the estancia.[18]

The evidence on rural landholdings demonstrates the well known fact that in-laws and relatives often cooperated with each other. The records on the estancia further indicate that Toro Mazote was bent on obtaining possession of contiguous parcels for a large estate. Owning an estancia was both a status symbol and a means of diversifying the family's economic base. To tend the crops and livestock, Ginés probably depended on poor whites and nonwhites, both free and enslaved. He eventually acquired an encomienda,[19] and thereby increased the size of his work force. His new rank as an encomendero did not, however, elevate him to the social level of encomenderos who held large grants of Indians. By the early seventeenth century, distinctions between mere vecinos moradores, who happened to obtain a writ of encomienda for a small group of Indians, and the highly placed vecinos feudatarios were fading, but the patricians did not relinquish their social preeminence.[20]

For the children of a notary to surmount the

built-in societal constraints, family ingenuity and resources would have to be mobilized. Ginés and doña Elena accordingly set themselves to the task of grooming their offspring for advancement. Not all of the Toro Mazote y la Serna children can be placed on a specific rung of the social ladder, but a general pattern of ascent did prevail.[21] If nothing else, the considerable success of the three sons and two daughters, who are treated in the chapters that follow, brought additional respect to the family name. This was largely achieved through education, public offices, and marital alliances.

Chapter 5

Moving Up

During their marriage, Ginés de Toro Mazote and doña Elena de la Serna together prepared the groundwork that their children used to good advantage. Some of them received additional help from their widowed mother after their father died in 1606.[1] The daughters and sons--doña Juana, doña María Magdalena, Ginés, and Andrés--all gained recognition and thus merit inclusion in the ensuing discussion. Because of the importance of his career and descendants, Manuel de Toro Mazote y la Serna warrants his position as the central figure in Chapter 6.

Doña Elena de la Serna was no doubt instrumental in arranging the marriage of her daughter doña Juana de Toro Mazote y la Serna to don Fernando Bravo de Naveda in 1624. Doña Juana's husband had seen active military duty in the south where his paternal grandfather ranked as a conquistador-encomendero and his maternal grandfather, a licentiate, served temporarily as the acting fiscal of the audiencia of Concepción. Don Fernando settled in Santiago and in

1623 signed a contract to purchase an allotment of black slaves in Buenos Aires and bring them to Chile for sale by his senior partner. Ten years later, don Fernando won election as the alcalde of moradores in the Santiago city council. Before he completed his term as magistrate and councilman in 1633, Governor Francisco Lazo de la Vega appointed him to the most prestigious office in the Central Valley, that of corregidor and deputy captain general of Santiago. His duties thus encompassed military defense in addition to hearing court cases as a district magistrate and presiding in the cabildo, where two of doña Juana's brothers served as councilmen.[2]

The attraction of city council posts for men in and affiliated with the Toro Mazote family was a long story. The notary Ginés, as we have seen, literally wrote the first chapter in that chronicle between 1585 and 1606 as the proprietary clerk of the cabildo. His daughter doña María Magdalena contributed more than a footnote when she married the peninsular Tomás de Olavarría, who owned the dual post of alderman and depositario general (public trustee). In this latter capacity, Tomás held in trusteeship any litigious property and received as compensation 3 percent of the value of the property. To insure its safekeeping during the litigation, he had to post bond. When he purchased the office in July, 1594, for 7,600 pesos of assayed silver, payable in three installments, it carried authority over Indian property. However, the crown revoked that power, Tomás no longer wanted the office, and it was put up for sale.[3]

After he stepped down, his father-in-law, the

notary Ginés, bought the office for his son and namesake, Ginés de Toro Mazote y la Serna, for 1,500 gold pesos in 1605. The notary's title to his own office did not refer to him as a hijodalgo, but Governor Alonso García Ramón, who supervised the sale of the trusteeship, accorded him that honor and noted that he had been in Chile for thirty-eight years. The governor required 2,000 gold pesos as bond for the trustee. Ginés, the younger, took office on September 9, 1605, and a vecino morador posted bond for him six days later. Philip III confirmed the purchase in December, 1607, by which time all vendible posts had been declared transferable in a decree which set the initial transfer fee due the royal treasury at one-half of the value of an office. For subsequent transfers, it was one-third. The crown's actions and his father's foresight assured young Ginés a lifetime tenure in the cabildo where he served actively for forty years. The transfer procedure kept the office in the family, with some interruptions, until 1720.[4]

Although Ginés de Toro Mazote y la Serna bought an estancia from his widowed mother, he had little success in getting and keeping an encomienda. As a morador, he belonged to the group of landowning cosecheros who produced tallow and hides and used their cabildo positions to influence export policies. On the local scene, the municipal meat market needed a supplier in 1622, and the city council accepted the public trustee's offer to furnish the beef for one year.[5]

In 1614 the cabildo named Ginés to a three-man committee to audit the accounts of the municipal hospital. That same year he was involved in two questions of precedence. The councilmen rotated the position of city inspector of local businesses, but whose turn came first not infrequently provoked debate. This was the case in 1614 when the proprietary councilmen and the aldermen elected as vecinos encomenderos jockeyed for position. To guarantee his place in the rotation order, the public trustee appealed to the audiencia of Santiago for a decision. Thereafter, he regularly took his turn inspecting shops carrying the staff of office of fiel ejecutor. Ginés lost in his bid to replace an alcalde, however. When the alcaldía fell vacant in 1614, the cabildo ruled against him and in favor of the elected alderman don Francisco de Zúñiga, a vecino encomendero.[6]

The trustee's failure to achieve encomendero status later set the stage for a heated quarrel in the cabildo. The incident developed in the following way. Governor Lazo de la Vega appointed don Gaspar de Soto, the alcalde of vecinos, to the office of corregidor and deputy captain general in July, 1630. It had become customary in such cases for an alderman to assume the alcalde's duties as a councilman and local magistrate. Four aldermen, including Toro Mazote, came forward as candidates for this vacant alcaldía in August. Although he garnered support from the alcalde of moradores and three regidores, his opponents forestalled a decision by arguing that it was not fitting for him to represent vecinos encomenderos and appealing the question to the audiencia. Since the high court dragged its feet, Governor Lazo de la Vega interposed his executive authority and in October appointed Toro Mazote to fill the vacancy until the cabildo would hold its regular, new elections on January 1,1631. Four councilmen heartily endorsed the appointment, two accepted it with the reservation that it not be considered a precedent against the rights of vecinos encomenderos, and one grumbled that the governor did not fully understand those rights.[7] Social considerations as well as local factionalism, political ambition, and gubernatorial favoritism had fueled the fire of the dispute.

Slightly different situations between 1633 and 1637 did not, however, occasion debate. On March 15, 1633, the cabildo named Ginés de Toro Mazote as the temporary replacement for his absent brother-in-law don Fernando Bravo de Naveda, the alcalde of moradores. In September, the latter became the corregidor, and Ginés filled out his term in the alcaldía. During his term as corregidor, Bravo de Naveda left the city four times and carefully observed precedent and protocol in naming the alcalde of vecinos as his substitute.[8] By respecting the minor differences between prominent moradores and the more prestigious vecinos, Bravo de Naveda avoided controversy.

During Ginés de Toro Mazote's tenure as a "perpetual" councilman, he entered another lifetime contract when he married doña Inés de Córdoba y Morales in 1627. As a descendant of conquistadores through both the paternal and maternal lines, she held a rank superior to that of her husband. In accepting his proposal, doña Inés, however, probably placed more weight on financial considerations and potential security than on social standing. Widowed once, if not twice, before she married Ginés, she had three children to consider as she made her decision.[9]

Her choice proved to be beneficial for her descendants. For instance, don Pedro de Salinas y Córdoba, her son by Alonso de Salinas, succeeded his stepfather in the city council. The youth married the public trustee's niece, doña Francisca de Toro y Celada, on May 1, 1644, and before Ginés died in 1645, he renounced his office in don Pedro's favor. The renunciation included a proviso that his own young son don Matías de Toro y Córdoba would obtain the public trusteeship upon coming of age. Don Pedro took office in December, 1645. The fee on this initial transfer amounted to 2,500 silver pesos, one-half of the assessed value of the post. Since a royal tax (medianata) was imposed on the first two years of proprietorship, don Pedro paid not only the transfer fee but also the tax of 125 pesos for the first year and posted bond for the second payment. Moreover, bondsmen pledged surety of 8,000 pesos for his faithful discharge of the trusteeship. His half brother Matías duly acquired the office in 1662. It was now appraised at 7,000 pesos, and don Matías therefore paid 2,333 pesos, 3 reales as the fee on this second transfer and the medianata of 116 pesos, 6 reales. He also reimbursed don Pedro for the initial transfer fee of 2,500 pesos and an additional 500 pesos that had been spent to secure royal confirmation of don Pedro's ownership of the office.[10]

Don Matías proved less conscientious in this

regard and failed to meet the deadline for securing crown approval of his title to the trusteeship. When the audiencia, at the instigation of an alert fiscal, declared the office vacant and for sale in 1674, don Matías purchased it for his eighteen-year-old son with the right to exercise it himself until the boy Ginés was of legal age to do so. This prerogative cost him 500 pesos that he paid immediately in cash along with the medianata of 79 pesos, 1 real, but he was allowed to pay the remaining 4,000 pesos of the purchase price in three equal annual installments. The oidores who conducted the sale routinely enjoined him to obtain royal confirmation of the bargain he had struck.[11]

Whether don Matías did so is a moot question because of lacunae in the cabildo records. However, a son-in-law, Martín González de la Cruz, the husband of doña Francisca de Toro y Eraso, appeared in the council as the public trustee from 1687 to 1697. An interim depositario named don Matías de Toro y Córdoba, either the former proprietor or his son, exercised the office until the end of the century. González de la Cruz had regained it by 1707 and owned it until he died in 1720, but an acting public trustee replaced him in 1718 because he had not posted bond. It is quite probable that the Toro y Córdoba heirs contested the monetary value of the office--if not its possession--when they sued each other over the division of the paternal estate.[12]

The direct cost of the office including purchases, renunciation fees, medianatas, and the expenses of obtaining royal confirmation constituted a sizable financial outlay for the power and prestige of owning an ex officio city council post. Notwithstanding the expense, occasional family acrimony, and interrupted tenures, the Toro Mazotes had dominated the public trusteeship since 1605 when the notary Ginés bought it for his son and namesake. Unlike the son-in-law Olavarría, who stepped aside after a brief term as the trustee, this branch of the family maintained a tenacious hold on the office for more than a century.

The family had also established ties with seventeenth-century proprietors of the cabildo office of alférez real (royal standard bearer, ensign). On August 27, 1654, don Matías de Toro y Córdoba, the future trustee, married doña Beatriz de Eraso y Ubitarte, the daughter of the alférez don Francisco de Eraso and doña Blanca de Ubitarte, a Peruvian. Don Francisco owned his place on the council from 1618 until he died in 1671. His son don Domingo became the alférez through the transfer process in 1683 and retained possession until the end of the century.[13] The Toro-Eraso marriage thus forged a bond between these bureaucratic families.

Although the Chilean Erasos were on a slightly higher social plane than the Toro Mazotes, the families were similar in origin. Moreover, they had a common interest not only in local government but also in rising to encomendero status. Don Francisco obtained a writ of encomienda for two lives in 1649 and registered royal confirmation of the grant in the cabildo records four years later.[14]

Don Matías de Toro y Córdoba and his sister doña Apolinarda also had grants of Indians. The title to her encomienda was called into question, however, in 1696. Her son then sought to regain it, citing the merits and services of his forebears. His list included Ginés de Toro Mazote y la Serna, the public trustee, and doña Francisca Ricardo de Montalbán, the wife of a former high court judge in Santiago.[15] This great-grandson of the <u>oidora</u> (wife of an oidor) thus utilized a tried and true technique for demonstrating prestige and filing a claim on royal gratitude.

Even the short-lived court in Concepción, as previously mentioned, embellished family trees because of the marital alliances between colonists and audiencia ministers. Since the high court of Santiago was destined to last for two hundred years, its imprint on both society and government would be more pervasive. With its employees, some of whom purchased their offices, and its ministers, a fiscal and a panel of judges, the audiencia had its own hierarchy that participated in the judicial and administrative processes. Its creation also set in motion a small and slow yet steady stream of new people in high places who were often accompanied by their wives and family members. It was this court that brought doña Francisca Ricardo de Montalbán to Chile where her progeny married into the middle and upper ranges of society.

Doña Francisca came to Santiago with her second husband Doctor Gabriel de Celada, a member of the original bench. They embarked for his assignment with their children, her sister, and six servants. Her son by a previous husband sailed with them from Spain, and it was his grandson who entered the plea for the Toro y Córdoba encomienda in the 1690s.[16] Earlier, the arrival of the oidor's entourage and the inauguration of the high court in 1609 had a profound effect on the personal life and professional career of Andrés de Toro Mazote y la Serna, a brother to the public trustee Ginés.

As a youth, Andrés earned the licentiate degree in Lima and returned to Santiago to practice law. He was the eldest son of the notary Ginés de Toro Mazote and doña Elena de la Serna and therefore inherited his father's encomienda in 1606. During her son's student days, the Indians worked for doña Elena, and she compensated him with money and real estate, including an estancia.[17] His encomienda, property, education, and especially his profession brought Andrés to the attention of the audiencia and the Celada-Montalbán family.

When the judge died in office in 1614, the widowed oidora obtained the guardianship of their two children, don Alonso and doña Luisa de Celada, who were still minors. A year later, doña Luisa received a dowry worth 7,000 pesos to marry the licentiate Andrés de Toro Mazote. In his last will and testament drafted in 1649, Andrés asserted that he also had 7,000 pesos at the time of the marriage. This document and doña Luisa's will of 1656 reveal that the couple raised sheep and goats, operated a mill and a tannery, and produced wine on several pieces of real property. As laborers or servants, Andrés had thirty black slaves and thirteen Indian slaves. The latter were in addition to the Indians of the encomienda that their eldest son don Pedro de Toro y Celada inherited. Since he was under age when Andrés died, doña Luisa represented him in matters regarding the encomienda. In 1641, her daughter doña Gabriela, who was promised a dowry of 14,000 pesos, married don José de Riberos y Figueroa y Aguirre, a descendant of conqistadores of Chile and an oidor of Charcas. The bride whose baptism took place in 1617, was the godchild of the corregidor of Santiago, Juan Pérez de Urasandi.[18]

Although the licentiate Andrés and doña Luisa had a large family, at least two of the children did not survive infancy. It was their daughter doña Francisca who married don Pedro de Salinas y Córdoba, the stepson of Ginés de Toro Mazote, the public trustee. Uncle Ginés served as godfather for his niece doña Antonia de Toro y Celada in 1625. A maternal aunt, doña María de Celada, and her husband, the corregidor of Santiago don Fernando Carvajal y Ulloa, acted as godparents for her niece doña Ana María in 1624. Other relatives and friends chosen as baptismal sponsors for the Toro y Celada children included the notary Manuel de Toro Mazote, the secretary of the audiencia Bartolomé Maldonado, his wife doña Nicolasa Suárez Fortuño, and, last but far from least, Governor Lazo de la Vega.[19]

Financial resources, prestigious marriages, and prominent friends helped this branch of the Toro Mazote family make visible social progress, but the licentiate Andrés also gained recognition through his public career. While his brother Ginés functioned as the public trustee, the licentiate held appointive and elective positions. For instance, Governor Alonso de Ribera commissioned him to act in a judicial capacity in 1612 and 1614. In the first of these appointments,

Andrés was authorized to hear cases concerning military personnel. The warrant from Governor Ribera dated May 15, 1612, did not list any illustrious Toro Mazote forebears. It did, however, stress that the attorney had the necessary qualifications and learning to hold the post of auditor general of the royal army in the kingdom and thereby exercise jurisdiction over civil and criminal cases involving either soldiers or officers. Since he would have to give up his private practice in order to serve His Majesty in this judicial office, Andrés would receive a salary of 400 ducats as budgeted in the royal military subsidy for the Chilean army. The warrant was to be publicly announced and recorded in the minutes of the Santiago city council. In copying the document, the cabildo clerk certified that the town crier had read it verbatim before a large crowd of people in the plaza on May 17. As auditor general, Andrés accompanied the governor to the Araucanian country but soon returned to Santiago. There on July 29, 1614, he received his second appointment from Governor Ribera. This was a more routine commission and merely empowered him to preside over the judicial investigation of an ex-corregidor's term of office (residencia).[20]

The cabildo chose the licentiate as the city procurator in 1615 and the municipal attorney in 1618. Between 1615 and 1622 he frequently substituted for absent corregidores, including his compadre Juan Pérez de Urasandi. He was an elected local magistrate and city councilman as the alcalde of moradores in 1616 and 1622.[21]

During his second term as an alcalde, Andrés

suffered a minor setback that may have soured him on local politics. In 1622 he and other council members clashed with the audiencia over a jurisdictional question that is examined more fully in the next chapter. Although the licentiate Andrés de Toro Mazote ran afoul of the high court on that occasion, he had reached the apogee of his career as a practicing attorney in the early 1620s when he was the acting fiscal of the audiencia.[22]

Notwithstanding his overall success, Andrés could never quite live down his family background, and there were those ready to remind him of it. When his compadre Governor Lazo de la Vega, who had already shown favoritism to the licentiate's brother and brother-in-law, nominated Andrés and two others as vecinos encomenderos in 1636, the city councilmen, with the exception of the alcalde of vecinos Diego Cárcamo Valdés, approved. The alcalde thought that underhanded dealings caused the governor to elevate the three men above the many other residents who had the appropriate "quality" for becoming vecinos.[23]

Diego Cárcamo Valdés was, to all appearances, something of a fortune hunter. Although he ranked as a vecino, it was his affluent patrician wife, doña Ana María de Azoca, who held the title to an encomienda.[24] Having married into the prominent Azoca family, the alcalde resented the recognition accorded to a licentiate, married to the daughter of an oidor. Andrés de Toro Mazote, because of his law degree and marriage, had risen farther and faster than any of his siblings. Yet his success provoked a comment that reaffirmed the old concept that quality was inborn, not acquired. An attorney with a distinguished wife and an encomienda was not universally accepted as a vecino.

Chapter 6

A Wealthy Notary

If the licentiate Andrés and the public trustee Ginés de Toro Mazote y la Serna stood in the often flattering but sometimes unfavorable glare of the public limelight, their younger brother Manuel was content to maintain a lower profile and work more unobtrusively behind the scenes. It is therefore more than a little ironic that Manuel amassed a fortune that enriched his descendants in the later colonial period. His father, the notary Ginés, made a long term investment in Manuel's future by renouncing his own office in the youth's favor on August 8, 1606.[1]

When the notary Ginés de Toro Mazote died later in 1606, it appeared that the transfer of his office might fail to win approval from the governor and treasury officials then supervising proprietary offices. The treasury officials actually went so far as to accept a bid of 3,000 gold pesos from a prospective buyer. Doña Elena de la Serna did not intend to see her young son Manuel lose his patrimony by default. She accordingly intervened on his behalf by sending her son-in-law Tomás de Olavarría to argue that the office was transferable to Manuel and not for sale by the crown officials. After seeking the advice of an attorney, Governor Alonso García Ramón ruled in favor of Manuel's claim on the office. The treasury officials appraised it at 2,000 gold pesos, despite the higher bid just tendered, and accepted 666 pesos, 5 tomines, and 4 grains as the transfer fee from Manuel on January 27, 1607. The governor issued a title to the office on March 20 in Concepción. On April 7, Manuel took the title to the Santiago council chamber where the cabildo accepted it, noting that he could begin to function as a notary and the cabildo clerk when he attained his twenty-fifth birthday. The notary who recorded the cabildo minutes that incorporate this documentation was Manuel's maternal uncle Melchor Hernández de la Serna.[2]

Five years later Manuel returned to the cabildo on December 29, 1612, with royal confirmation of the gubernatorial title to the office and certification that he had been born on December 25, 1587. Since he was now of legal age, the council formally received him as a notary and the cabildo clerk. He would continue to function as the clerk until November, 1661.[3]

From that vantage point, Manuel de Toro Mazote y la Serna observed his brothers and their colleagues debate and make decisions on municipal affairs. Since he simultaneously maintained a private notarial practice, he knew the ins and outs of everything worth knowing in the Central Valley. Quietly he filed away bits and pieces of information useful for his various enterprises that yielded a fortune estimated in excess of 70,000 pesos when he died at the age of eighty-three years in 1670. During his long life, Manuel acquired three large estancias and raised livestock. He owned both Indian and Negroid slaves. One of the slave women, Isabel, gave birth to an illegitimate daughter who was duly baptized in 1634. The baptismal record for the child Juana unfortunately fails to mention her mother's race and omits the father's name. Manuel, the slave owner, also obtained a writ of encomienda, engaged in the Chilean-Peruvian trade, made a business trip to Buenos Aires in 1633, and served as the tithe farmer for the diocese of Santiago in 1635.[4]

The notary-rancher-businessman had so many professional and financial interests that he had little time to express his private opinions. However, he received a formal charge from the cabildo to draft an official report on the disastrous earthquake that struck Santiago and its environs on May 13, 1647. This was an unusual opportunity for Manuel to compose a document rather than set down the resolutions passed and ordinances proposed in the council. His account reflected the climate of opinion of his day that included a religious perspective. Thus he viewed the earthquake as a threat from God's "divine justice" and a sign of his "infinite mercy" in "miraculously" sparing the lives of many Chileans in spite of the fact that "our sins justly" merit punishment. Through the intercession of Our Lady and the many religious men and women in the city's convents, God deigned to pity sinners but did not spare them from the loss of their homes. Although some said the earth shook for half an hour, Manuel agreed with those who thought the first and most severe quake lasted for fifteen minutes. He asserted that aftershocks continued until June 1. Over 600 persons of all ranks had died in the city and countryside, and large and small buildings that had been constructed over the course of a century lay in ruins. In that scene of desolation, Bishop Gaspar de Villarroel had proved himself a worthy spiritual leader by preaching an on-going sermon and consoling his people. Manuel concluded his report with a remark that it was written as a reminder to posterity and as an act of thanksgiving to God.[5]

The calamity that the earthquake and a subsequent typhoid epidemic visited upon Santiago preoccupied the cabildo and its clerk for months. As the work of rebuilding the city gradually progressed, petitions to the viceroy and the king brought relief from newly imposed royal taxes. Manuel de Toro Mazote meanwhile overcame any losses he had suffered. In the 1650s, he and a business associate operated a store in Santiago. They also exported commodities and at least seven slaves to Lima. Manuel was among the landowners who sold provisions for the garrison at Valdivia in 1653 and 1654.[6]

As a youth, this wealthy man had the sobering experience of watching his widowed mother struggle to repay his father's debts. He was fully aware of the costs of educating his brother Andrés, acquiring the public trusteeship for Ginés, and getting and keeping the notarial office that he and his father held. Perhaps it was for these reasons that he became a penny pincher in regard to obtaining his due for his work in the city council. In any event, he campaigned doggedly to collect his annual salary of 200 pesos and periodically reminded the councilmen to furnish him with paper and ink for the cabildo records.[7]

Manuel and his brother Ginés took working-vacations to supervise the yearly slaughter of livestock on their rural properties. When the cabildo temporarily banned the slaughter of sheep in the 1620s, the brothers were among those granted licenses to do so on a limited scale.[8] There was nothing illegal in this. It is nonetheless a sign of their ability to capitalize on their positions within the council to advance their private financial interests.

The notary Manuel, unlike his brothers the public trustee and the licentiate, did not marry above his social station. Since his wife doña Juana de Cifuentes Hidalgo held a rank similar to his, the marriage did not represent a significant social advance for either of them. Her father's name, Simón Díaz Hidalgo, might connote hidalguía, but he was a mere ciudadano when elected to a term as an alderman in 1605. Her widowed mother, doña Francisca de Cifuentes, provided the bride with a dowry worth 8,000 pesos in 1621, however.[9] The marital endowment helped Manuel become a successful stockman and merchant, yet he continued to ply his profession as a notary public.

The papers that crossed Manuel's desk are worthy of close scrutiny because of the information they hold on the texture of colonial life. (Appendix 3 consists of documentary abstracts from his notarial ledger.) When he and his fellow notaries receive the specialized, comprehensive treatments they deserve, the history of Chile and its capital will be more fully understood. For present purposes, however, a less extensive examination of his ledger must suffice. Among the possible avenues of exploration, the most feasible at this time is to isolate a brief moment in his long career and develop a case study of his clients and their activities within the context of the times. The early 1620s are a particularly apt focal point. Manuel, recently married, had a decade of professional experience behind him and was hard at work in both the cabildo chamber and his private office while his brothers were following their public careers. This was, moreover, a period of considerable agitation that accelerated the pace of colonial routine. As the clerk of the cabildo, Manuel recorded the minutes of the city council meetings, known as the Actas del cabildo, that will serve as an introductory guide to those eventual years. The minutes for the weekly sessions held in the 1620s are typical of the Actas throughout the Hapsburg era in that they give full, detailed coverage to some items of business and prove exasperatingly vague on others.

In providing a perspective for viewing Manuel's work and clientele, it is easier to describe his city then to enumerate its population. Accurate census figures simply do not exist; the Actas contain only a few, unreliable statistics; and modern demographers have yet to apply their scientific tools to other raw data that have survived. In spite of these problems, scholars have compiled estimates on the number of people in the colony at large, and it would appear that the population of Chile in 1620 numbered approximately 15,000 whites, 40,000 hispanized mestizos, 22,000 blacks and dark-skinned persons of racially-mixed origins, and 480,000 Indians with slightly more than half of the Indians living in the unpacified regions. Roughly contemporary descriptions of Santiago suggest that it had almost 400 houses, but over 60 residences were of poor quality. There were some 550 adult white males, excluding diocesan priests and members of religious orders. Two convents housed more than 120 nuns. Over 300 white married women resided in the city, but data on other females are regrettably too fragmentary to hazard numerical guesses about them. Within Santiago's jurisdiction, the total urban and rural Indian population, counting men, women, and children, probably ranged between 6,000 and 9,000 including 400 to 500 artisans who lived in neighborhoods on the outskirts of the city. These craftsmen worked as tanners, shoemakers, tailors, potters, blacksmiths, stonecutters, masons, carpenters, and house painters; a few engaged in weaving silk and making rope from hemp. Most of the Indians, nevertheless, continued to live in the countryside, either as villagers long since allocated in encomiendas or as workers on white-owned chacras and larger rural estates. Although some encomenderos still assigned their tributaries to the placer mines, the sixteenth-century gold bonanza had largely spent itself. The Central Valley was self-sufficient in terms of food production because nonwhites and poor whites tilled the fertile soil and tended livestock. In addition to the cereals, vegetables, fruit, wine, meat, and fish available for local consumption, Santiago produced wheat, hemp, tallow, and hides for export to Peru or shipment to the army in the south. Textile workshops (obrajes) turned out coarse woolen cloth. While much business was conducted in direct producer to consumer exchanges, over 40 small retail establishments handled a variety of merchandise and groceries.[10]

When the residents of Santiago crossed the large central plaza on their way to and from the shops, government buildings, and churches, or paused for a call in a friend's home, they talked as people always do of their immediate, personal concerns. If they chanced to consider the Chilean topics most publicized outside the colony, they spoke of the Araucanian war and the related issue of Indian status. In their narratives, colonial chroniclers devoted considerable space to the military history of the frontier. How to conduct the war was and would continue to be a question debated in the royal and viceregal councils on the basis of reports from Chile. Similarly, debate raged on the rights and duties of the Chilean Indians. Given the nature of colonial government, the Hapsburg monarchs bore the ultimate responsibility for policy decisions on these grave matters. As Philip III neared the end of his reign and Philip IV assumed the awesome task of administering the Spanish domains, they faced the dilemmas emanating from their distant realm.[11]

Their loyal vassals in the Santiago cabildo maintained their traditional stance favoring a war of conquest against the Araucanians who should be subdued with "fire and blood" wielded by soldiers paid and supplied by the crown. Prisoners of war should be condemned to slavery. These arguments, coupled with the dauntless Araucanian resistance, had won concessions from Philip III in the early seventeenth century when he authorized a military subsidy, a small standing army, and the enslavement of captives. The royal subsidy pumped additional money and goods into the Chilean economy while Araucanian slavery enlarged the labor pool. Pro-Indian advocates, however, had convinced the king to institute a defensive military strategy that unfortunately proved short-lived. In learned treatises and the halls of government, they also condemned both slavery and the abuses of encomienda Indians. Their efforts secured the enactment of the Tasa de Esquilache, a major piece of reform legislation, in 1620. However, the clauses outlawing Indian slavery and restricting encomienda labor met stout resistance from the vested interests in and represented by the Santiago cabildo. For example, when the city council called for legal steps to suspend the enforcement of the Tasa in March, 1621, the royal treasurer and alderman Jerónimo Hurtado de Mendoza cast the only dissenting vote. As the crown endorsed first one and then another policy, it was impossible to predict the outcome of the contest between the pro- and anti-Indian forces. The latter, nevertheless, undermined the campaign on behalf of encomienda Indians and delayed the formal abolition of Indian slavery until late in the seventeenth century.[12]

The upper classes voiced their opinions on the

war and the Indian through the cabildo. Speaking as their representatives, the council urged the crown to finance and furnish the manpower for an offensive war to crush Araucanian depredations. The vecinos themselves could not and should not be called up to fight because they were too few in number, they and their forebears had already contributed so much military assistance that they had impoverished themselves, and the crown had previously granted them an exemption from active duty in the south. Unless the king sent soldiers and weapons, the war, plus the threat of English corsairs seizing the southern coast, would bring about the total ruin of the colony. Total ruin would also ensue if encomenderos lost the right to exact personal service from their Indians. As the descendants of conquistadores, the vecinos merited rewards for generations of service to the crown. These same vecinos, although impoverished, could always find money to pay lobbyists to present their petitions and protests in Lima and Spain.[13] In framing their case, the upper classes had, in a sense, collectivized the arguments that individuals used in requesting compensation for merits, services, and need.[14]

Just as a vassal pledged unswerving fealty to his monarch, so too the cabildo manifested loyalty to the Hapsburgs. When news arrived in 1622 of the death of Philip III and the accession of Philip IV, the councilmen first donned mourning, paid for out of city funds, to grieve for the dead king in January and then participated in the public ceremonies honoring the new sovereign in June. The cabildo was delighted to join in the joyous cries of "long live the king." It was considerably less enthusiastic in its reaction to Philip IV's appeal for financial help to repel his enemies who were not only attacking on European battlefields but also striking at the maritime lifeline to the Indies. After discussing the fact that Chile was poverty-stricken, the council, in effect, tabled the king's request.[15] To have done otherwise would have negated the carefully constructed argument from poverty that appeared in the city's petitions for favors.

The cabildo's relationships with viceroys, governors, and audiencia ministers who represented royal authority tended to follow a pattern of cooperation until some dispute disturbed the calm. The latter was the case in the 1620s when the councilmen felt particularly wronged and threatened by the Prince of Esquilache's measures on behalf of the Indians. As his term as viceroy drew to a close, the cabildo gathered charges to use against him in his residencia. Don Fernando de Irarrázaval was active in this regard.[16]

Rapid turnovers in the Chilean governorship during the Esquilache viceregency not only hampered the enforcement of the reforming Tasa but also complicated the political scene. When Governor Lope de Ulloa y Lemos died in office in December, 1620, the senior, and for the moment only, oidor in the audiencia succeeded him. Doctor Cristóbal de la Cerda y Sotomayor began his provisional governorship with a certain urgency. In a hastily called meeting of the city council on December 13, 1620, a Sunday afternoon,

Cerda took the oath of the office in Santiago. He was not wasting any time in claiming his legal right to become governor after news of Ulloa's death arrived from the south on December 12.[17]

The oidor's motives for moving so fast are attributable in part to his ambition. Cerda, a Mexican creole, had studied in Spain where he married doña Sebastiana de Avendaño y Villela and received an appointment as a judge in the high court of Santo Domingo. They were embarking on a thirty-year odyssey when they sailed for the island post with their young son in 1615. Only two years later, the crown named Cerda an oidor of Chile, and their troubles began in earnest. In the Caribbean, their ship was captured by English pirates, who seized slaves that don Cristóbal had with him and took doña Sebastiana's dowry that was reputed to be between 20,000 and 30,000 ducats. At least one source credits the oidora, who was pregnant, with persuading the pirate leader to spare her husband's life. After they were put ashore in Central America, she delivered the child. When they reached Peru, the archbishop of Lima helped them financially, but Cerda fell seriously ill with a disease that ate away his nose. The exhausting and nerve-wracking journey ended in 1619 when the disfigured judge arrived in Santiago with his wife and children. A year later, Governor Ulloa died; Cerda's only colleague, the licentiate Fernando de Machado, was in Lima; and don Cristóbal had a golden opportunity to add to his list of services to the crown in his role as acting governor. After many petitions for favors, he finally won promotion to the audiencia of Lima as a criminal judge in 1636. But the crown decreed his retirement in 1638 because of deafness. When he died in 1645, the high court of Lima granted doña Sebastiana one-half of his annual salary to cover his funeral expenses.[18]

The experiences of the star-crossed oidor and oidora were sufficient to explain his eagerness to assume the interim governorship in 1620. Cerda's motivations nevertheless probably included a genuine sense of duty. He was the only high ranking official present in Chile, and rumors were circulating that his predecessor had been murdered. Cerda therefore launched an investigation of Governor Ulloa's death. The interim fiscal of the audiencia, the licentiate Andrés de Toro Mazote, called for the inquest that led Cerda to suspect doña Francisca de la Coba y Lucero, the widowed First Lady, of poisoning her husband; no charges were ever proved, however.[19]

The fiscal also alerted Cerda to a violation of a royal cédula of December 12, 1619, that forbade chief executives to use their patronage to favor their relatives, clients, and friends. Governor Ulloa had disobeyed the decree by appointing a member of his household, the treasury official Juan Bautista de Ureta, to the office of corregidor of Santiago. Cerda therefore declared Ureta ineligible and named don Fernando de Irarrázaval as corregidor and deputy captain general. The details of don Fernando's appointment became clear on January 15, 1621, when he presented his letter of appointment to the dual post. He had taken office earlier in a rare night meeting on December 14, 1620. The cabildo had allowed him to be sworn in and receive the staff of royal justice after his bondsmen Alonso Cid Maldonado and the licentiate Juan de Morales Negrete routinely pledged surety for him. The special session was in response to an executive order from Cerda which stated that the formal appointment was being drafted. Although don Fernando was absent from the city from time to time, he remained in office until October, 1621. This meant that he was the titular head of the cabildo when Governor Cerda made his initial efforts to implement the Tasa de Esquilache. Bitter, lingering conflict between Cerda and the city council was the chief result of his attempts to enforce the Indian legislation.[20]

The cabildo looked forward to welcoming a new governor in 1621, and made the customary arrangements to present don Pedro Osores de Ulloa with a horse and saddle. Once Osores took office, Cerda returned to his duties in the high court and began to prepare an información on his governorship. When the cabildo raised a formal objection to some of his claims, the judge vented his anger in a face-to-face confrontation with the alférez don Francisco de Eraso in 1623. Cerda insulted Eraso personally, called the councilmen villains, and said that he had made a mistake in not having them beheaded while he was governor. Eraso responded that the cabildo was not composed of traitors but of "very loyal vassals of His Majesty." After the council was informed of the spiteful exchange, it resolved to fight back in the audiencia. As the suit progressed in the high court, the cabildo appointed the licentiate don Alonso de Celada, the son of a former oidor and brother-in-law of Andrés de Toro Mazote, to the salaried post of city attorney to replace an unsatisfactory lawyer. The council renewed its feud with Cerda in 1636 when he was undergoing a residencia prior to leaving for his post in Lima. Those voting to press charges included Eraso and the public trustee Ginés de Toro Mazote.[21]

During his administration, Governor Osores had altered the Tasa de Esquilache in such a way as to remove regulations that the encomenderos found most onerous. The cabildo approved; the audiencia objected. Osores then suspended the enforcement of both the original Tasa and his amended version. Philip IV tried to end the stalemate with a royal decree of 1622 that incorporated much of the Tasa but included a clause once more legalizing the enslavement of Araucanian prisoners of war.[22]

The seventeenth-century Actas are thus a faithful mirror reflecting the highly significant, recurring issues concerning the war and the Indian and the interaction between the cabildo and the higher authorities. These same records also reveal the city council busily performing a wide variety of roles and functions that from time immemorial have pertained to municipal governments. Among these, public works projects loomed large.

Three major projects were underway in the 1620s-- a breakwater on the Mapocho River designed as a flood prevention measure, work on the city hall (casas del cabildo) and municipal jail, and a bridge over the Maipó River that like the famous structure in London had a propensity for falling down--with the first claiming the most attention. The overall supervision of the breakwater rested on the shoulders of don Pedro Lisperguer. When Governor Cerda appointed him to the job, the cabildo enthusiastically endorsed him in a rare instance of cooperation with the official who became the council's adversary. Since workers were indispensable for labor-intensive construction, Indians were predictably assigned to the task. Some came from the local environs; a few were moved from the north; others were brought from the trans-Andean province of Cuyo. Cabildo discussions of wages for the workers make it doubtful that they were ever fully paid. The wage due each Indian was, in any case, a mere fourteen pesos for eighteen months work. The Indians did, however, receive food and clothing. A special tax was levied to finance the breakwater, but collection and accounting procedures were, to say the least, primitive. Several councilmen, including don Fernando Bravo de Naveda and the public trustee Ginés de Toro Mazote, handled the funds. Ginés also figured in appraising the value of cordovan leather, grogram cloth, tallow, food, and oxen that some taxpayers remitted in lieu of cash payments. The materials to build the breakwater included stone, timber, lime and iron tools such as axes and adzes. Carts to transport the supplies, oxen to pull the carts, and fodder to feed the oxen were also needed. Items were purchased with tax revenues or requisitioned from local residents. In the case of one Luis Rodríguez, the owner of a yoke of oxen that somehow became lost after being requisitioned, the council voted to pay for the animals. The minutes do not report an ox roast taking place at the construction site.[23]

As the breakwater neared completion in 1622, the cabildo remarked that the Cuyo Indians could soon be assigned to work on the city hall. Prior to this, a kiln had been built to fire the tile and bricks necessary for the structure while prisoners from the jail, mainly Indians, made bricks by the thousands and worked on both the jail and city hall.[24] The building and repairing of public works would continue with fluctuations in the degree of interest the projects generated. As previously explained, much rebuilding had to be done after the earthquake of 1647.

Other routine cabildo duties included the review of credentials. The task of recording the materials in the Actas of course fell to the cabildo clerk. Governors as well as district and local officials submitted their letters of appointment. Manuel de Toro Mazote also copied militia commissions, certifications that men had received holy orders, and, from time to time, royal decrees. Livestock owners who registered their brands with the clerk of the council thereby attested to the rural orientation of the economy.[25]

The Actas reported a slight, but permanent, change in the composition of the city council in 1622. Until that time, the two royal treasury officials, who purchased their positions, were ex officio aldermen. After the crown revoked their membership in the council, the seats were sold to new proprietors. This represented a setback for the cabildo because it had tried but failed to purchase the privilege of electing two aldermen to replace the treasurer and accountant.[26]

The cabildo records were officially closed to outsiders. As an historical source, however, they are somewhat analogous to periodicals devoted to news coverage. In tracing events, it soon becomes apparent that both a rich ceremonial life and a round of more mundane activities characterized the colonial capital. The former featured not only the special festivities staged in honor of a new king or governor but also the elaborate services held annually during Holy Week that marked the regular passage of time for a people of religious faith. While the city councilmen enjoyed honorific recognition in these observances, they wielded authority on the local level. Setting prices and standards of commodities continued to be a cabildo responsibility, backed up with the right to inspect municipal shops. Regular inspections of the hospital and precautions to ward off contagious disease also claimed the cabildo's attention. In the 1620s, the council discussed epidemics that might spread to Santiago if black slaves being brought through Cuyo from Buenos Aires entered the city. Slave importers caught the council's eye as a possible source of revenue, but the audiencia evidently vetoed a proposed tax on the slavers. Even the children of the city came within the council's purview. For example, the cabildo appointed a public guardian (<u>padre de menores</u>) in 1620 to care for poor orphans and see to their training. A search for a teacher to instruct young boys in the Three R's apparently proved successful in 1621.[27]

All of these varied aspects of city life

influenced Manuel de Toro Mazote and the clients who called upon him for his professional services. In his private practice as a notary and his public office as cabildo clerk, he encountered a cross section of society and demonstrated that he was fully cognizant of class and caste. Blacks and Indians, for instance, were designated as members of those racial groups. Although he was meticulous in citing military titles, these offer little assistance in evaluating an individual's precise social status because of the proliferation of militia commissions in the seventeenth century. It is also true that men of the likes of "Captain" Juan Gómez had worked long ago to dilute the older meaning of military titles. The anomaly of an increasingly civilian society in the Central Valley clinging to martial honors would continue. Meanwhile, the notary preserved a more accurate indicator of social standing in the records he kept: in both his notarial registry and the city council minutes, he held the line on the use of don. For example, he did not presume to apply the title to himself, his father, or his brothers but did refer to his mother as doña Elena de la Serna. The private papers he handled concerned patricians respectfully identified as dons and vecinos encomenderos, political officials and bureaucrats, women from the upper through the lower ranks of society, professional men, merchants doing business with Lima and importing black slaves from Buenos Aires, commoners engaged in a variety of craft and retail operations, as well as laborers and servants, both free and enslaved, white and nonwhite. Ecclesiastics and religious orders also figured in the transactions that Manuel handled.[28]

As the following inventory of his registry reveals, the documents Manuel notarized between August, 1622, and February, 1623, spanned a wide range of endeavor, most often of a straightforward financial or economic nature.[29] The ledger, like the Actas, thus opens a window on his world. Two established procedures in a notary's work extend the time period in some cases beyond the stipulated six months. In the first place, receipts canceling debts or other obligations were often recorded in the margins of the original document. Secondly, it was sometimes necessary for a notary to insert copies of previous documentation in order to validate a position or transaction.

In terms of sheer numbers, Manuel notarized more powers of attorney than any other single category of papers. The twenty-one poderes covered diverse subjects, however. There were the predictable authorizations to handle financial affairs. Persons who needed an agent in another locality, especially merchants engaged in the Lima trade, issued these and frequently instructed the proxy to make purchases and pay debts. Several powers of attorney authorized proxies to draft a last will and testament in the event of the death of the party issuing the document.

Two powers of attorney concerned the Araucanian war, specifically remittances due from the royal military subsidy. The first of these, dating from October 24, 1622, sought payment of 4,310 pesos in freight charges owed to Antolín Sáez de Galiano, a vecino morador who owned a ship that had carried supplies to the frontier. The second, recorded on January 10, 1623, referred to an allotment of merchandise purchased from Pedro del Portillo for 8,125 pesos, 3 reales and transported to the island of Chiloé. The goods included fabrics, stockings, hats, scissors, needles, thread, axes, adzes, and iron. The authorization for payment came from an *acuerdo de hacienda*, a special meeting of the governor, fiscal of the audiencia, and treasury officials.

A week later, Portillo, who owned a store in Santiago that was obviously capable of a large volume of business, obtained a power of attorney to collect 4,314 pesos in fines, damages, and court costs levied against the posthumous estate of Governor Alonso de Ribera in the residencia following his term as governor of Tucumán. Portillo paid for this right with money and with goods from his store on January 17, 1623. Ribera had died in office in 1617 during his second term as governor of Chile[30] before the Council of the Indies issued its verdict on his administration in Tucumán. When the ruling of February 13, 1620, reached Tucumán, Ribera's bondsman paid the 4,314 pesos. A local official in Tucumán then reimbursed the bondsman and traveled to Chile to collect the sum from the dead governor's assets and heirs. Rather than pursue the matter in person, he issued the power of attorney to Portillo. The standard practice of posting bond and conducting a residencia had thus produced some complex and protracted aftereffects.

This case presented Manuel de Toro Mazote with an object lesson on gubernatorial liabilities. He had just had the opportunity of observing his most prestigious client, Governor Pedro Osores de Ulloa, a knight of the Order of Alcántara, exercise a prerogative of high office. On January 13, 1623, don Pedro had commissioned his son and doctor Pedro Machado to plead at court for favors from the king. In this way, the governor prepared to collect a fringe benefit for his service in Chile.

Since Osores de Ulloa died in 1624, he failed to reap any personal compensation from his messengers' efforts. Doctor Machado, however, evidently made himself known at court. Like his father before him, he was promoted from the post of fiscal to that of oidor of the Santiago high court.[31]

When Machado was planning his trip to Spain in 1623, the vecino encomendero don Diego González Montero named him in a power of attorney as one of three proxies to petition the crown for rewards in remuneration of the services he and his forebears had rendered. Don Diego, a native-born patrician, eventually became the acting governor of his homeland, which was a rare privilege for a creole. In 1622 and 1623 he was settling an urban real estate transaction and trying to win a lawsuit that would increase the number of his Indian tributaries. In regard to the latter, he appointed a solicitor to act for him and issued a power of attorney to be used in Santiago to advance the encomienda case. His opponents in the suit regarding the Indians of Pelvín were the brother and sister, doña Isabel and Antonio de Azoca, a treasury official. In still another power of attorney, don Diego appointed his wife, mother, stepfather, and three other persons not only to manage his encomienda and handle his property but also, if he should die, to draft his will. His longevity obviated this last proviso, however.[32]

Andrés Jiménez de Lorca, a peninsular who became a vecino morador in Santiago and obtained an encomienda in Cuyo, had need of a personal agent in that trans-Andean province after Governor Osores de Ulloa appointed him to the post of protector of Indians in Santiago. Manuel de Toro Mazote copied the letter of appointment into the Actas on April 7, 1622.[33] In the following January, he notarized Jiménez de Lorca's power of attorney that placed Juan de Silva Vargas in charge of the Cuyo encomienda for one year with the understanding that he would be paid in Indian labor and tribute.

The protector visited Toro Mazote's office in his official capacity on January 10, 1623, when he approved a power of attorney from the sailor Juan Ramos, a Peruvian Indian from Cuzco. The document delegated a priest to represent Ramos in proceedings to annul his marriage to the Indian woman María, who belonged to the encomienda of don Francisco Rodríguez de Ovalle.

Indian agents, including the protector as well as the corregidores of districts subject to Santiago and the administrators of Indian villages, had to post bond because they handled Indian property.[34] The Toro Mazote registry contains seven instances of bondsmen pledging surety for the minor bureaucrats. In four of the cases, the protector Jiménez de Lorca was on hand to certify that the bond was adequate.

To insure good work and compliance with municipal ordinances, some artisans and retailers also had to post bond. As a result, bondsmen came to the notary Manuel on behalf of three tailors and a shopkeeper who ran a <u>pulpería</u> (shop that sold wine and staples). While he was taking his turn as the city inspector of local businesses in September, 1622, the public trustee Ginés de Toro Mazote approved the bond that was posted for two of the tailors. The cabildo not only licensed and regulated pulperías but also sold contracts for supplying the city with fish and meat. Rodrigo López and Bernabé Gallegos hotly disputed their rights regarding the fish and meat markets until they settled their differences in a notarized agreement on November 15, 1622.[35]

During the 1620s, the crown was requiring foreigners to buy permits to reside in the Indies,[36] and this provided more business for Manuel de Toro Mazote. Three aliens regularized their status by promising to pay the fee of 200 pesos each in installments to the royal treasury office in Lima. Two of these men were Portuguese sailors from the ship <u>San Bernabé</u> anchored in the port of Papudo and bound for Peru.

The notary had gone to Papudo with a copyist he employed and also notarized papers for Juan de Santiago, who owned and captained the <u>Santo Tomás</u> that was taking on cargo for the Lima trade. These documents indicate that this merchant and his partner employed one Pedro Seco to sell their merchandise in Chile.

As the following examples show, Juan de Santiago

and other merchants often had to extend credit to their customers. Part of Pedro Seco's job was to collect 1,924 pesos, 7 reales still owing on merchandise he had sold for the total price of 14,564 pesos. The first 200 pesos he collected would pay his salary which was in arrears.

Another merchant, Juan Bautista de Casas, held a promissory note for some 300 pesos, due and payable within one year, from Luis de Toro Mazote, a brother to Andrés, Ginés, and Manuel. Their maternal uncle, Gaspar Hernández de la Serna, who was related by marriage to Manuel's wife,[37] had purchased grogram yardage from Andrés de Zamudio for 150 pesos. On August 17, 1622, Gaspar promised to pay the debt in silver or livestock commodities, specifically tallow or hides. If commodities were used, they would be valued at the prices in effect at the end of March, 1623. An increase in the price of tallow and hides would thus benefit Gaspar and reduce the profit margin for Andrés; a fall in prices would reverse the circumstances. On October 11, 1624, Andrés issued a receipt acknowledging payment in full but unfortunately failed to give details on how he had been paid. His agreement with Gaspar nevertheless hints at a type of speculation somewhat akin to the modern practice of bidding on commodity futures.

Gaspar's son-in-law Gonzalo Ferreira y Aponte, whose wife was a first cousin to both Manuel and doña Juana de Cifuentes, entered a credit agreement with an even more pronounced speculative element. In September, 1622, Francisco de Toledo y Arbildo, a landowner who purchased one of the cabildo seats vacated by the treasury officials, pledged all of the tallow he would produce by the middle of April, 1623, to repay a debt of 700 pesos to Gonzalo. The sum evidently represented the value of goods purchased from the latter's store. Francisco promised to deliver the tallow, in bags marked with his identifying brand, to a Chilean port and to abide by the price that would be in effect at the time of delivery. Gonzalo accepted these terms and stated that if the tallow were worth more than 700 pesos, he would pay Francisco the difference.[38] Gonzalo was obviously playing the role of a middleman as a tallow buyer with an eye on the export sector of the economy. He and Francisco were each willing to take their chances on the future market value of a livestock commodity to settle a debt.

Payments in kind and installment payments were common in seventeenth-century Chile because of a chronic currency shortage.[39] This helps to explain why businessmen had to resort to credit when dealing with each other. On September 23, 1622, a local merchant promised to pay the importer Sebastián de Tapia 636 pesos, 6 reales for goods he had already received, including a ream of paper costing 5 pesos. On the same day, Tapia issued a power of attorney to a Lima resident to acquire new merchandise worth 8,000 pesos.

To meet their financial needs and cope with the monetary problem, some individuals who bought on credit or borrowed money had to find a bondsman to furnish surety or surrender promissory notes they held. The former could be effected rather simply; for example, a bondsman served as the underwriter for the repayment of a debt of 150 pesos that don Sancho de las Cuevas Villaroel owed to Juan Luis de Medina. The latter could become more complicated. Thus a merchant named Juan Fernández de Montoya, who held promissory notes worth a total of 882 pesos from two individuals, used both documents as surety for repaying 1,000 pesos that he borrowed from Juan Andrés de León.

Property owners who needed to raise capital had another option: they could obtain cash loans through censos guaranteed with real estate. To be legally binding, the documents had to be notarized. The Toto Mazote registry contains one censo held by a private individual and others pertaining to nunneries.

Among the latter is the censo for 2,000 pesos that Juan de Ahumada Gavilán and his wife doña Juana de Cáceres owed to the Santa Clara convent. For their daughter doña Juana[40] to take her vows as a nun, they paid a dowry of 2,000 pesos. The abbess then loaned them that same sum, not in cash but in three gold chains, as a censo in August, 1622. As collateral for repaying the principal and meeting the interest payments of 100 pesos per year, they pledged urban and rural property. Receipts dated 1649 and 1651 canceled all or part of the financial obligation. The arrangements evidently proved satisfactory to all parties concerned. Doña Juana had taken her place as a professed Clarisa nun; her parents had endowed her yet retained 2,000 pesos as working capital at the low rate of 5 percent simple interest; the convent had made a safe, guaranteed investment; and the notary, who had gone to the nunnery to authorize the document, had earned his fee of 12 reales.

Another case concerning dowry-censos may have caused some grumbling among the Augustinian nuns. The nunnery had to relinquish four censos it held as the dowry for doña María Cid Maldonado when she left that convent to become a Santa Clara nun. The Augustinian abbess nevertheless transferred the documents that represented some 2,000 pesos to the syndic of the Santa Clara convent on November 19, 1622, before the notary Manuel de Toro Mazote.[41] This time his fee was only 8 reales.

In addition to the dowries payable at the time a woman made her profession of vows, the nunneries, at least the Santa Clara convent, required small payments for the food and living expenses of novices. Don Juan de Valenzuela, who placed two daughters in that convent,[42] accordingly promised to remit 120 pesos annually, in the form of livestock, during their novitiate.

Lengthy documentation, all notarized by Manuel de Toro Mazote over a period of seven years, incorporated papers concerning the Santa Clara nuns doña Clementa and doña Beatriz de Escobar y Torres as well as their family and its associates.[43] Their father was the merchant Alonso de Escobar y López. When he died in Lima in 1615, several of the children were underage and his encomienda devolved upon his son and namesake who was approximately five years old. Alonso del Campo Lantadilla, the chief constable of Santiago and executor of the decedent's will, therefore thought it advisable to have a legal guardian appointed.

The constable presented his request to the

licentiate Andrés de Toro Mazote, who was substituting for the corregidor, on November 3, 1615, emphasizing that the guardian would manage the encomienda and defend the boy's interests in lawsuits regarding the Escobar estate. A widowed mother did not automatically assume legal custody of her children, and, as Campo noted, Escobar's widow doña Luisa de Torres was doubly impeded. He was referring not to the fact of her illegitimate birth but to her participation in the litigation. He did not have to explain to a magistrate trained in the law that a widow could sue in the courts to defend her rights to half of the community property and to her parental dowry-inheritance. After hearing from the constable, the licentiate Andrés sent his brother Manuel, the notary of record in the corregidor's court, to consult with doña Luisa. She nominated Alvaro Rodríguez, who married Escobar's half sister, and the magistrate confirmed the appointment, stipulating that Rodríguez would be the tutor and guardian of the persons and properties of the Escobar y Torres children during their minority. Doña Luisa and two men posted bond for Rodríguez before the notary Manuel, who also recorded the guardian's oath to fulfill his duties. Andrés de Toro Mazote, still substituting for the corregidor in December, 1615, formally authorized the tutelage and guardianship.

By July, 1616, doña Luisa had died, and her daughters who entered the Santa Clara convent were completing their novitiate. Since they were ready to profess, the Franciscan friar functioning as the <u>padre guardián</u> of the convent gave them permission to make their wills and thereby dispose of their earthly possessions. The procedures of granting the licenses and executing the wills took place in the convent parlor in the presence of the abbess doña Elena Ramón and the ubiquitous Manuel de Toro Mazote.

The wills were separate but almost identical documents. Each novice made a pious donation of sixty pesos to the convent and stipulated that the payments for her support during her novitiate, as shown in Rodríguez' ledgers, and her dowry were to come from her paternal and maternal inheritance. Doña Beatriz bequeathed the residue of her estate to Rodríguez while her sister doña Clementa left hers to Alonso del Campo Lantadilla.

In September, 1617, Campo ceded his inheritance from doña Clementa to her brother-in-law Inocencio Martínez de Aparicio, the husband of doña María de Escobar y Torres. Before he did so, he deducted 222 pesos, 1 real that included the cost of material for nuns' hoods that he had given to doña Clementa. The itemized assets transferred to Inocencio listed the black slave woman Violante first. Since the two nuns owned the slave jointly, she would continue to work for both of them during her lifetime, but the sum of 200 pesos representing half of her monetary value figured in the inheritance consigned to their brother-in-law. Doña Clementa's share of a censo that Campo had invested with the proceeds from a sale of urban real estate equaled 190 pesos, 2 reales. Another censo with a principal of 1,000 pesos plus the interest that was not yet paid would also go to Inocencio along with 136 pesos, 2 reales that debtors owed the Escobar y Torres heirs. Their guardian Alvaro Rodriguez was in charge of collecting the latter sum. The value of the family residence, when divided among the children, added 927 pesos, 2 reales to doña Clementa's assets that totaled over 2,000 pesos. In transferring his rights to the inheritance, Campo enjoined the new beneficiary to invest the money in censos and use the income as doña Clementa would direct. The chief constable also mentioned that he had given Inocencio further instructions on the ultimate disposition of the inheritance after doña Clementa's lifetime.

All of the preceding documents were transcribed under the date of September 23,1622, when Alvaro Rodriguez and Inocencio Martinez de Aparicio issued a power of attorney to be used in Lima to collect debts owed to Alonso de Escobar's posthumous estate. The two men had a personal interest in the proceedings because they were acting as the heirs of the two nuns. Rodriguez was also fulfilling his duty as a guardian while Martinez de Aparicio was representing doña Maria de Escobar's claims on the paternal estate. To demonstrate his right to do so, he had the notary certify that he and Maria were indeed husband and wife.

The material on nuns in the Toro Mazote registry thus sheds a few rays of light on nunneries. The Escobar y Torres papers also serve as example of the function of the court of the corregidor in appointing legal guardians and the process of settling parental estates. With its references to debts in Lima, the power of attorney emphasizes the financial and economic ties between Santiago and the viceregal capital.

The documents also had a then unforeseeable kinship implication because descendants of Inocencio Martínez de Aparicio and doña María de Escobar later married into the Toro Mazote y Cifuentes family. Alvaro Rodríguez, his wife doña Isabel Suárez, and doña Magdalena del Campo Lantadilla, the illegitimate daughter of the chief constable, would all play supporting roles as events moved to unite the families.[44]

At the moment, with ships making sail for Peru, the practical world of business demanded attention. Since Rodríguez and Martínez de Aparicio needed agents to collect from the Escobar y Torres debtors in Lima, their power of attorney named the busy merchant Juan Bautista de Casas as a proxy on September 23, 1622. The previous day, as Casas made final preparations for his business trip to Peru, he visited the notary Manuel to prepare a power of attorney for two fellow merchants who would handle his affairs in Santiago. One of the proxies was Inocencio Martínez de Aparicio. Since the canons of the notarial profession required Manuel de Toro Mazote to mention the status or occupation of individuals, this document identifies Martínez de Aparicio, the husband of a merchant's daughter, as a merchant himself.

If this documentation underscores the importance of the Pacific trade and the market economy centered in Lima, bills of sale and exchange that Manuel de Toro Mazote processed indicate the significance of Buenos Aires as a port of entry for Negroid slaves.

Officially closed to commerce during much of the Hapsburg era, Buenos Aires became a major center for contraband trade, much of it in human cargos from Africa and the Portuguese colony of Brazil. Other Negroid slaves, of course, entered Chile through Peru.[45]

Toro Mazote's ledger names his future brother-in-law don Fernando Bravo de Naveda, his cousin by marriage Gonzalo Ferreira y Aponte, the chief constable Alonso del Campo Lantadilla, the constable's son-in-law don Juan Cajal, Bartolomé de Rojas y Puebla, Juan Andrés de León, and Alonso Bello as Chileans who imported slaves. It incorporated seventeen bills of sale or exchange involving twenty-five slaves, both black and mulatto, old and young, male and female. Although Chileans had little compunction in buying, selling, and trading slaves, newly-imported Africans, known as bozales, were described as prisoners taken in a "just war" and thereby subject to perpetual servitude.[46] Debates on the morality of Negroid slavery did not become a matter of legal record in the notary's office.

The documents state that a mulatto woman came from Libson, a mulatto boy from Lima, one black man from Spain, and another from Biafra but identify Angola as the homeland of the majority of blacks. This was true of transactions involving Toro Mazote's relatives. For example, María, an Angolan, was approximately 20 years old when Rojas y Puebla sold her for 450 pesos to the priest Gabriel de Cifontes (sic), an uncle of the notary's wife.[47] Toro Mazote's mother figured in a transaction with Juan Flamenco who ceded her his young Angolan slave, Lucrecia, because doña Elena de la Serna manumitted his mulatto daughter Andrea. As she released the child from bondage, doña Elena explained that she owned Andrea's mother and appreciated the slave woman's services. Since the children were between 7 and 8 years of age, doña Elena obviously expected to profit from Lucrecia's lifelong servitude. Don Fernando Bravo de Naveda, who soon married doña Juana de Toro Mazote y la Serna, obtained 1,040 pesos from the sale of 4 slaves, including an Angolan mother and her young children Ana and Domingo whom he sold to doña Catalina Justiniano.

Some bills of sale called for immediate payment in cash or in kind. In several cases, however, the buyer promised to pay the agreed upon price within a set time period while the seller retained a lien on the slave. Those calling for deferred payment in an export commodity again point to market speculation. The following examples more fully illustrate how individuals bought and sold slaves during this time.

Doña Aldonza de Guzmán, twice widowed,[48] bought 2 young Angolan women for 900 pesos but deferred payment for 6 months. She purchased the slaves from Alonso del Campo Lantadilla who held a lien on them until the price would be paid in full. The women had been brought to Santiago from Buenos Aires by Bartolomé de Rojas y Puebla for Campo Lantadilla and his partner Gonzalo Ferreira y Aponte. The same partners also sold 4 other Angolans for 1,810 pesos payable within 6 months, half in silver and the other half in tallow. The tallow would be evaluated at the prevailing future price. The purchaser was don Gaspar de Soto who acted through a proxy who held his power of attorney and served as his bondsman for making the payment. In a simpler sale, don Cristóbal Pizarro paid for the Biafran slave Domingo, who was about 20 years old, with 470 pesos worth of hemp priced at 17 pesos per hundredweight. The seller in this case was San Juan de Hermua.

The licentiate Francisco Maldonado de Silva, a physician,[49] participated in two transactions involving four slaves. In the first of these, he sold his black slave Domingo del Narijado, born in Spain, for 212 pesos, payable within 2 months and traded his mulatto slave woman from Lisbon for a black Angolan woman and an additional 50 pesos. The terms of the second transaction are not entirely clear. However, it assigned a value of 250 pesos to Francisco, a mulatto born in Lima and between 9 and 10 years of age, when the physician acquired him. The document also mentioned medical expenses due for the treatment of the deceased Governor Lope de Ulloa. The executor of his posthumous estate evidently received a payment order to cover the medical bills from the widow doña Francisca de la Coba. The executor--who was Juan Bautista de Ureta, the disappointed candidate for the office of corregidor in 1620--then deeded young Francisco to Maldonado de Silva in lieu of cash payment.

Not only Negroid slaves but also free blacks and mulattoes formed an important contingent in the multiracial urban and rural work force largely comprised of Indians. While city council protests against legislation favoring Indian workers occupied much of Manuel de Toro Mazote's time in his official capacity as cabildo clerk, his private notarial practice reflected a dispute between the audiencia and city council that arose over labor contracts and directly affected his brothers, the licentiate Andrés and the public trustee Ginés, in 1622.

The cabildo became incensed in October when the high court ruled that the Tasa de Esquilache gave oidores, rather than local magistrates, the power to authorize Indian labor contracts. To signify their disgust with the audiencia's usurpation of local authority, the corregidor don Pedro Lisperguer and the alcaldes don Gonzalo de los Ríos and Andrés de Toro Mazote resigned their posts on October 8. The high court had them arrested for showing disrespect to the offices. A magistrate exercised royal jurisdiction; hence a resignation was an affront to the king. The audiencia then ordered the council to elect new alcaldes. The cabildo had already voted to appeal the question of Indian contracts to the Council of the Indies but reluctantly complied with the court order and chose the alférez don Francisco de Eraso and public trustee Ginés de Toro Mazote as alcaldes. The crown ultimately ruled against the oidores and in favor of local officialdom. Notaries, in the meantime, continued to record contracts between employers and working people from the several ethnic groups.[50]

Between August and November, 1622, Manuel de Toro Mazote transcribed seven such agreements. Four of these were in the nature of apprenticeships. Before they resigned their offices, the alcalde Toro Mazote and the corregidor Lisperguer apprenticed three youths to become a barber, a tailor, and a shoemaker. Similarly, the new alcalde Eraso authorized Jacinto, a mestizo, to learn the trade of silk weaving. The oidores Gaspar de Narváez y Valdelomar and Fernando Machado, on the other hand, put Indians named Bartolomé, Martín, and Luisa to work. The cartwright Bartolomé entered a contract to make and repair carts for Alonso de Salinas. Martín and Luisa became servants. The latter's contract was of particular interest to Manuel de Toro Mazote and his wife doña Juana de Cifuentes Hidalgo because Luisa was going to work for her aunt, doña Ana Félix de Cifontes, who was married to Manuel's uncle, Gaspar Hernández de la Serna. The notary therefore obligingly promised to compensate the servant if Gaspar failed to do so and to provide her with room and board.[51]

While Manuel's pledge pointed to the enduring strength of family ties, his professional contacts also helped to pave the way for the forthcoming marital alliance between the Toro Mazote and Córdoba y Morales clans. The head of the latter family, the encomendero Alonso de Córdoba, an aged patriarch,[52] was putting his affairs in order and summoned the notary to his chacra near Santiago on October 1, 1622, to record four documents. He acknowledged an obligation to Juan López de Córdoba, perhaps a relative through an illegitimate line, and deeded him rural land on the Pacific. The rest of Alonso's coastal land, along with its herd of 200 cattle, went to his son Ambrosio, who also received title to another estancia. The value of the land given to Ambrosio totaled 1,100 pesos; the cattle at 12 reales a head were worth 300 pesos. Both of these sums were to count as part of Ambrosio's maternal and paternal inheritance. The final document was Alonso's promissory note to pay 200 pesos for a set of weapons that he bought for Ambrosio.[53] The younger man was planning a trip to Spain, not a tour of duty against the Araucanians, however. Ambrosio therefore granted his brother-in-law Alonso de Salinas a power of attorney to handle his affairs during his absence.

Salinas, the husband of doña Inés de Córdoba y Morales, owned land adjoining Ambrosio's estancia on the seacoast and had witnessed the documents his father-in-law dictated. In addition to hiring the Indian cartwright mentioned previously, Salinas rented out an apartment in his city residence for the sum of ninety pesos a year. Both he and the tenant signed the lease that Manuel de Toro Mazote recorded on August 19, 1622. In November he was in the notary's office with the licentiate Andrés and the trustee Ginés de Toro Mazote to witness a power of attorney from his brother-in-law Diego de Morales y Córdoba to their brother Luis. In that document, Diego authorized Luis to act for him, write his posthumous will, and serve as his executor. Alonso de Salinas was an elected alderman at the time, but the cabildo noted that illness prevented him from taking his turn as city inspector in December, 1622. He died in 1624, and his widow doña Inés de Córdoba y Morales soon married the public trustee Ginés de Toro Mazote.[54] As already explained, her sons by Salinas and Toro Mazote went on to hold the public trusteeship.

Although some clients made it a point to provide one or more of the witnesses for their transactions, others relied upon finding them in Manuel de Toro Mazote's office. Since his fellow notary Antonio de Bocanegra was a frequent witness to documents, the two men probably worked in the same quarters. Antonio was a Peruvian who had moved to Santiago and presented his credentials as a fully authorized notary to the city council in November, 1621.[55] Thereafter he substituted for Manuel as cabildo clerk from time to time. They were on friendly terms because Antonio rented a house from a master tailor for two years in 1623 for an annual rent of sixty pesos, and Manuel notarized the lease gratis.

Two other real estate leases, four land deeds, and a marital endowment with its subsequent receipts for installment payments round out the papers that Toro Mazote handled during the period under consideration. His usual fees ranged from six to twelve reales--scant remuneration for preserving a valuable microcosm of political, economic, and social life.

It should be borne in mind, however, that neither notarial nor cabildo records are a foolproof index to the colonial social register. Because of their legalistic nature, these written sources fall short of total reliability as a lexicon. Innuendoes that might be found in less formal writing such as personal correspondence and in conversation are missing. Marriage and baptismal records also have their limitations. The following examples nevertheless provide data on offspring, relatives, and friends of the Toro y Cifuentes household.

When the notary Manuel and doña Juana pledged their marriage vows and doña Juana received the nuptial blessing in 1621, their attendants were the merchant-encomendero Juan de Astorga and his wife doña Beatriz Navarro. The latter was the sister-in-law of the chief constable Alonso del Campo Lantadilla. Since the notary and his wife were both first cousins of doña Luisa Hernández de la Serna, they were logical choices to act as godparents for her son in 1624. Doña Luisa and her husband Gonzalo Ferreira y Aponte, the merchant, were baptismal sponsors for her namesake doña Luisa de Toro y Cifuentes in 1630. The patriciate furnished sponsors for two other Toro y Cifuentes children. Don Gonzalo de los Ríos and his wife doña Catalina Lisperguer y Flores, the godparents for young Simón in 1636, were patricians but less aristocratic than don Jerónimo Bravo de Saravia, who was the alcalde of vecinos when he became Francisco's godfather in 1623. Two years later, Gabriel de Toro y Cifuentes was baptized, and his parents soon began to rear don Jerónimo's illegitimate daughter who was the same age.[56]

Don Jerónimo's presence among the baptismal sponsors for the Toro y Cifuentes children furnishes an apt illustration of the continuing divisions between and within the intermediate and upper classes. He was a compadre to his godson's parents but the revered forebear of latter day Irarrázavals who were the offspring of the Bravo de Saravia-Irarrázaval marital unions.[57]

Establishing compadrazgo and amicable relationships with members of the old elite was as far as the notary Manuel and doña Juana could go. Since they both had middle level rather than aristocratic familial connections, they had advanced but stopped short of reaching the patriciate. Diligent attention to the duties of a proprietary official combined with ambition and wealth, especially assets invested in land, nevertheless prepared the way for their descendants to acquire a symbol of elite status, an entailed estate known as a mayorazgo, in the eighteenth century.

EPILOGUE

While Manuel de Toro Mazote scratched away with his quill pen and amassed his considerable fortune, the lines separating merely affluent landowning encomenderos from the vecinos feudatarios who formed the patrician elite became blurred but were not erased. Mario Góngora who has examined the two groups finds few differences between old and new families as of 1655. The groups were similar in power and prestige, he maintains, but individuals within the groups occupied diverse political and social planes.[1] It is this last point that bears further consideration in regard to the Irarrázaval and Toro Mazote families.

Góngora correctly places don Antonio de Irarrázaval y Andía and his mother doña Antonia de Aguilera y Estrada among the descendants of sixteenth-century aristocrats and categorizes Manuel de Toro Mazote as a product of upward social mobility.[2] As we have just seen, the notary did prosper and gain recognition. His marriage and public life were not on a par with those of his brothers Andrés and Ginés, however. The latter's branch of the Toro Mazote family continued to own the public trusteeship into the eighteenth century, but the notary's line took only a passing interest in political careers. Although the peninsular Juan Antonio and Juan Luis Caldera exercised public offices, these men, who were the husband and son of doña Luisa de Toro y Cifuentes, soon turned away from politics. The elder Caldera did not bear the title don during his term as alcalde of moradores in 1695. The notary Manuel's grandson, Andrés de Toro Hidalgo, who called himself don, was content with one term as a magistrate and city councilman.[3]

In their struggle to get ahead, the notary Manuel and his wife doña Juana achieved substantial progress. Their son Andrés de Toro y Cifuentes wanted more. Like his forebears, Andrés nevertheless had to settle for a spouse from his own social stratum. His future bride, doña Antonia Hidalgo y Aparicio Escobar was the daughter of the peninsular Gaspar Hidalgo, who became a morador of Santiago, and doña María de Aparicio y Escobar, a member of the merchant family identified as clients of the notary Manuel in the preceding chapter. At her baptism in 1644, doña Antonia's godparents were doña Magdalena del Campo Lantadilla and her second husband, the chief constable Antonio de Barambio.[4]

Doña Antonia was in her early twenties when she married Andrés de Toro y Cifuentes in 1666 with a dowry said to equal 15,000 pesos. That same year the bridegroom purchased rural land, slaves, and livestock from his father. Further real estate acquisitions made him one of the largest landowners in the late seventeenth and early eighteenth centuries. The laborers on his estancias included his encomienda Indians. Although Andrés had failed to attract a marriage partner from the patriciate, he hoped to perpetuate his wealth through the creation of a mayorazgo. In a codicil to his will in 1704, he therefore instructed that urban property in Santiago and an estancia in the province of Aconcagua should be entailed for his only legitimate son don Andrés de Toro Hidalgo and his descendants. If this line should be extinguished, the descendants of his sister doña Luisa de Toro y Cifuentes and her husband Juan Antonio Caldera would obtain the entail. In the thirty-odd years since the death of the notary Manuel de Toro Mazote, the rules on the use of don had relaxed to the point that his son Andrés could refer to himself and his son as dons in the codicil.[5]

As his parents' only heir and with no surviving legitimate issue of his own, don Andrés de Toro Hidalgo saw no reason to institute the mayorazgo. In 1706 he inherited a fortune estimated at 150,000 pesos, or more than twice the value of his paternal grandfather's posthumous estate. Genealogical information on his first wife doña Josefa de Marín y Riberos is too sketchy and confused to pin down her place in society. The incomplete data nonetheless suggest that some of her ancestors ranked higher than those of her husband. Don Andrés gave his second wife doña Ignacia Hidalgo 20,000 pesos in 1740 as a wedding gift (arras) that included, according to one account, a keyboard instrument similar to a modern piano. Since don Andrés and doña Ignacia were not only husband and wife but also first cousins through his maternal and her paternal line, they decided to block the creation of the entail. When don Andrés died as an octogenarian in 1749, his will disclosed that he had named doña Ignacia as the sole heir to his estate. This set the scene for a lawsuit between the widow and the Caldera family. The latter won the suit in 1752 and obtained title to the entail. In this way, lineal descendants of the notary Manuel de Toro Mazote, doña Juana de Cifuentes Hidalgo, and their daughter doña Luisa took control of an estancia that the notary had purchased in the seventeenth century.[6]

Money and property had oiled the cumbersome machinery of social mobility and raised the stature of doña Luisa, her brother Andrés, and his son don Andrés.[7] However, they were still outside the inner circle of the old elite that boasted more honors and more exalted ancestry than they could muster. None of the three passed the crucial marital test that granted full membership in the patriciate. Their spouses were neither closely affiliated with high-ranking imperial officials nor, with the possible exception of doña Josefa de Marín y Riberos, descended from the conquistador aristocracy. If her status had momentarily elevated don Andrés de Toro Hidalgo, and it is not yet possible to ascertain that it did, his second marriage to his cousin doña Ignacia operated as a leveling factor. The litigation over the proposed entail, moreover, divided the family and no doubt left its scars.

While doña Ignacia Hidalgo fought the Caldera-Toro y Cifuentes claims to the mayorazgo and contributed to the family acrimony, she engaged successfully in another lawsuit. Her opponent was the nobleman don Miguel Bravo de Saravia Andía Irarrázaval, the marqués de la Pica. The verdict handed down in 1751 awarded her a piece of land that he had claimed. Her victory was not, however, a severe blow to don Miguel whose parents had entailed specified Bravo de Saravia properties, that came to be known as the Irarrázaval mayorazgo, for him in 1728.[8]

As his title and family names indicate, don Miguel's lineage reads like a roll call of distinguished patricians. Several of his Bravo de Saravia forebears have already been introduced. The following résumé will highlight Irarrázaval activities prior to the marqués' generation.

The powerful Irarrázavals of the seventeenth and eighteenth centuries owed much to women who graced the family tree. Not the least of these was doña Antonia de Aguilera y Estrada. By virtue of her hereditary merits and services, she was awarded an encomienda in Quito in 1614. Before her marriage to don Fernando de Irarrázaval and after his death, she was the encomendera of Rapel and Pacoa. When she died in the 1660s, their grandson obtained a renewal of the writ for the Chilean encomienda. Doña Antonia herself was the civil, titular administrator of the village of

Rapel by gubernatorial appointment in 1630. The pueblo had a cacique and a few residents as late as 1667. The ledgers of the protectors of Indians for 1614-1618 and 1637-1639 state that deposits in its caja de comunidad totaled 1154 pesos. The villagers sold sheep and cheese worth 304 pesos in 1622.[9]

Ten years later, don Fernando died in Arequipa, Peru, where he was the corregidor, the last in a series of appointive and elective positions he held. For example, he and doña Antonia had been newlyweds when he took office as the corregidor and deputy captain general of Santiago in 1620. As was customary, his letter of appointment from acting Governor Cerda cited his merits and previous services and those of his father don Francisco de Irarrázaval, the king's gentleman, as evidence of his qualifications for this combined post. Needless to say the document mentioned don Fernando's greatest personal distinction, his membership in the Order of Alcántara.[10]

During his brief tenure as corregidor, the contrast between don Fernando and the humble, yet respectable cabildo clerk Manuel de Toro Mazote, who had routinely recorded the official appointment in the city council minutes, was further underscored. The former received a writ of encomienda entitling him to half of the tributaries from a vacant encomienda in La Serena. Acting Governor Cerda issued the document in Concepción on February 12, 1621. He authorized don Fernando to bring the Indians and their wives and families to Santiago where the male tributaries would work on the city hall and jail that were damaged by flooding in 1620. After this they would help build the breakwater on the Mapocho River. Cerda justified the transfer of the Indians from the north to the Central Valley by explaining that the city of Santiago and its vecinos and moradores were too poor to bear the costs in terms of money and manpower of the important public works. Until these projects were finished, don Fernando would have to render an accounting of the Indians' wages, tributes, and labor to Cerda in his capacity as senior oidor of the Santiago high court. Only the king himself could divest don Fernando of the encomienda that would pertain to him and one successor, either a son, a daughter, or his widow according to the law of succession. The encomendero would, however, have to observe the special legislation on Chilean Indians that the Viceroy Esquilache had recently issued. On March 6, 1621, don Fernando took the writ to don Diego González Montero, the alcalde of vecinos, to be invested with the encomienda. With Manuel de Toro Mazote on hand to notarize the proceedings and don Salvador, a cacique, representing the Indians, the magistrate placed Irarrázaval in formal possession of the encomienda.[11] How long this endured the historical record does not say.

Don Fernando and doña Antonia had three sons and a daughter who survived to adulthood and whose baptismal sponsors included don Francisco de Ovalle and doña María Pastene y Lantadilla, a married couple who would become more important in Irarrázaval family history; the treasury officials Pedro de la Torre and Antonio de Azoca; and the latter's wife doña Isabel Guajardo. In 1637 the two older boys, don Francisco Fernando and don José, were en route to Spain. There don Francisco Fernando married his first cousin doña Francisca Antonia de Andía Irarrázaval, who obtained the noble title of vizcondesa from her father. Their cousin doña Lorenza de Sotomayor y Zárate, the marquesa de Villahermosa, later ceded them her title. From his mother's peninsular relatives, don Francisco Fernando inherited the Aguilera entail in Spain.[12]

The young Chilean émigré and his bride nevertheless wrote to doña Antonia de Aguilera for money in 1639. Her son praised his pretty wife and informed his mother that the "remote" kingdom of Chile was a good birthplace but less desirable as a place to live. Perhaps it was the realization that her brother-in-law don Francisco de Irarrázaval y Zárate, the marqués de Valparaíso, might enjoy prestige in Europe but lacked sufficient resources to support the newlyweds that prompted doña Antonia to decline their invitation to move to Spain. The letters did, however, reassure her about the progress her son don José was making in school, and her daughter-in-law stressed that good educational opportunities also awaited doña Antonia's third son don Antonio Alfonso.[13]

Notwithstanding the peninsular inducements, doña Antonia de Aguilera chose to remain in her homeland with don Antonio Alfonso and her daughter doña Catalina Lorenza. In 1644 the latter married don Juan Rodulfo Lisperguer y Solórzano, one of the most eligible widowers in the colony with a long list of civic offices to his credit. Through the maternal line, he was the grandson of an oidor of Santiago. His paternal forebears included: two Germans, Bartolomé Flores, a conquistador from the Valdivia era, and Pedro Lisperguer, who had come to Chile with doña Catalina Lorenza's grandfather after associating with him in the English court; and doña Elvira, the Indian headwoman of the village of Talagante that formed the core of the Flores Lisperguer encomienda. After twenty years of marriage, doña Catalina Lorenza, who bore no fewer than twelve children, died in childbirth, and don Juan Rodulfo then remarried. This patrician was therefore remarkable not only from the standpoint of his ancestry but also his progeny that numbered between twenty-two and twenty-five legitimate children.[14]

In 1649 don Antonio Alfonso de Irarrázaval replaced his brother-in-law don Juan Rodulfo as corregidor and deputy captain general of Santiago. As don Antonio Alfonso assumed his duties as presiding officer in the city council, the cabildo clerk Manuel de Toro Mazote recorded the letters of appointment. These papers emphasized the rank and deeds of the corregidor's paternal and maternal forebears as well as the status and achievements of his uncle, the marqués de Valparaíso.[15]

The notary Manuel de Toro Mazote knew only too well that he and his family could not rival the grandiose claims on the royal largess that don Antonio Alfonso had marshalled to win the appointive office from the governor. The documentation that don Juan Rodulfo submitted when he took office in 1648 reveals that he also recognized the superiority of the Irarrázaval y Aguilera family because it cites his marriage to doña Catalina Lorenza to enhance his personal and hereditary merits and services.[16]

In the seventeenth century, a man who sought a local or regional office did not usually call special attention to his wife unless the marriage demonstrated his social advance. Since don Antonio Alfonso's status was sufficient unto itself, his citations did not allude to his union with doña Nicolasa Zapata de Mayorga, the daughter of Francisco Zapata y Mayorga and doña Jerónima de Benavides. The marriage which took place in 1640 was, admittedly, more socially advantageous to her than to him because not all of her ancestors were particularly illustrious in spite of an early tie with a relative of Pedro de Valdivia. More recently, a collateral line merged with the Ovalle y Pastene family in the same generation that the latter effected a union with don Jerónimo Bravo de Saravia.[17] These connections plus doña Nicolasa's acceptability as a wife for an Irarrázaval indicate that she met the qualifications patricians set for marital partners. Don Antonio Alfonso's stature was so high and of such long standing that it compensated for any deficiencies in her background. Thus doña Nicolasa's marriage to don Antonio Alfonso should not be interpreted as a sudden move from one social orbit to another. Whatever slippage it occasioned for him was only minor because he went on to become a member of the Order of Alcántara.[18]

Don Antonio Alfonso and doña Nicolasa, moreover, arranged for their son don Fernando Francisco de Irarrázaval y Zapata to marry doña Agustina, who belonged to the rich, powerful, and prestigious Bravo de Saravia family of irrefutable patrician rank. The bride, whose ancestors included a governor and a conquistador, descended from don Francisco de Ovalle and doña María Pastene y Lantadilla, their daughter doña Agustina, and her husband don Jerónimo Bravo de Saravia. The bishop of Santiago conferred the nuptial blessing in 1670, and the bride's parents, don Francisco Bravo de Saravia and doña Marcela de Henestrosa, provided a marital dowry that carried a value of 40,000 pesos. Although it included an estancia, the endowment did not save the newlyweds from financial troubles, and don Fernando Francisco had to sell the land after doña Agustina's premature death in 1682. The estancia nevertheless remained within the Irarrázaval extended family because the purchaser was the husband of doña Catalina Lisperguer y Irarrázaval. Since the land was heavily mortgaged, don Fernando Francisco received little cash from the sale, and his finances continued on a downward plane. Family solidarity more than offset his managerial ineptitude, however. His mother doña Nicolasa Zapata paid his funeral expenses in 1690, and his wife's parents, now in possession of a title of nobility, the <u>marquesado</u> de la Pica, took charge of his eldest son don Antonio de Irarrázaval y Bravo de Saravia.[19]

By this time, the marqués and marquesa had weathered the storm of criticism that rained down on their daughter doña Catalina's marriage to Governor Francisco de Meneses.[20] Doña Catalina was presently living in Peru where her only brother don Jerónimo Bravo de Saravia died in 1685, leaving his daughter doña Marcela Norberta as the heiress to the title he would have inherited from his parents. In 1690 doña Marcela Norberta married her Chilean first cousin, don Antonio de Irarrázaval, and their grandparents the marqueses de la Pica guaranteed the young couple's financial future with the Bravo de Saravia encomienda, extensive rural lands, and the family residence in Santiago.[21]

After they obtained these assets, doña Marcela Norberta and don Antonio entailed the home and two estancias in 1728 for their eldest son don Miguel, the heir to his mother's title of nobility. The marquesa and her consort enjoined him and those of his line who would hold the mayorazgo, in conjunction with property entailed long ago in Spain, to use the surnames Bravo de Saravia Andía Irarrázaval and the coats of arms of both families.[22] The latter, of more elaborate ornamentation than the Caldera family's simple crest,[23] would serve as a visible reminder of venerable, illustrious lineage. Through his marriage to his cousin doña Francisca Portales y Meneses in 1730, don Miguel, the third marqués de la Pica, preserved that lineage.[24]

During two centuries of Chilean history, the social distance between the Irarrázaval and Toro Mazote families had narrowed but not disappeared. Once don Francisco de Irarrázaval and doña Lorenza de Zárate had established themselves in the colony, their patrician status served as a firm base for their descendants' continuing prestige. The forebears of the latter-day Toro Mazotes profited from commerce, the notary Manuel not only engaged in trade but also became an important landowner, and his son designed an entail. Manuel and his father relied upon the purchase and transfer of a notarial office to function in the lower level bureaucracy. The Irarrázavals flaunted their accumulated merits and services, and don Antonio Alfonso boasted of his titled uncle in Spain when he assumed the post of corregidor and deputy captain general in Santiago. After their merger with the Bravo de Saravia family, the Chilean Irarrázavals held entailed properties and a marquisate. As we have seen, doña Ignacia Hidalgo, the widow of don Andrés de Toro Hidalgo, won a lawsuit against the third marqués de la Pica at mid-eighteenth century.

A contemporary who remarked that the nobleman don Miguel suffered from hypochondria could nevertheless characterize him in 1762 as a "well educated, rich, and virtuous caballero."[25] This was a graceful compliment for the marqués, the product of an aristocratic lineage, constructed and preserved through marital alliances between members of the old elite. Across the generations, the Hernández, de la Serna, Toro Mazote, Cifuentes, and Hidalgo men and women found marriage partners within their own gradually ascending peer group. For these reasons, the proud Irarrázavals stood apart from the wealthy don Andrés de Toro Hidalgo whose family tree barred the doors to the inner sanctum of the patrician elite that money and property alone could not open.

Appendix 1

Abstracts of Church Records in Santiago 1583-1682

The Archive of the cathedral parish (archivo de la parroquia del sagrario) of Santiago, Chile contains records of baptisms, the exchange of marriage vows, and nuptial blessings known as <u>velaciones</u> from the early through the late Colonial Period. The Genealogical Society of Utah Library microfilms of the original manuscripts were consulted to prepare the following abstracts in English. Citations given below use acronyms for the archive, the pertinent volume, and the microfilm rolls.

Considerable liberties have been taken in translating and summarizing not only the parish records but also the documents compiled in Appendix 3. Essential features are stated in modern language with most of the repetitious legal formalities deleted. Names, especially surnames, have been added or deleted to make individuals recognizable to readers.

The body of information available from parish records will be useful to scholars in future demographic studies. The brief excerpts translated here merely accent the important steps of baptism and marriage in the family and religious life of colonial Chile. The documentation on wedding attendants and baptismal sponsors attests to associations, including compadrazgo.

A. Baptismal Record of Diego de Irarrázaval y Zárate.
(APS, BMV, Book III, f 167v, GL 797289)

Diego, the legitimate son of don Francisco de Irarrázaval and of doña Lorenza de Zárate, his wife, was baptized in the cathedral of Santiago on October 20, 1583. The godparents were Alonso Campofrío de Carvajal and doña Mariana de Riberos, his wife.

B. Marriage Certificate of don Alonso de Sotomayor and doña Isabel de Zárate.
(APS, BMV, Book III, f 158, GL 797289)

On January 12, 1590, in the pueblo of Curimón, Father Juan Varas, the _provisor_ (ecclesiastical judge) and vicar general of the diocese of Santiago, officiated at the marriage and nuptial blessing of don Alonso de Sotomayor, governor and captain general of this kingdom, and doña Isabel de Zárate. The attendants were Ramiriáñez Bravo de Saravia and doña Isabel Osorio de Cáceres, his wife.

C. Baptismal Record of Alonso de Sotomayor y Zárate.
(APS, BMV, Book III, f 113, GL 797289)

Alonso, the legitimate son of the Governor and Captain General of this kingdom, don Alonso de Sotomayor, and of doña Isabel de Zárate, his wife, was baptized in the cathedral of Santiago on June 25, 1591. The godparents were captain Ramiriáñez Bravo de Saravia and doña Isabel Osorio de Cáceres, his wife.

    D.   Baptismal Records of Antonio Alfonso and José de Irarrázaval y Estrada.
        (APS, BMV, Book IV, f 26, GL 797289)

Antonio Alfonso, the legitimate son of don Fernando de Irarrázaval y Zárate and of doña Antonia de Aguilera y Estrada, was baptized and anointed with oil and chrism on June 24, 1624. The godparents were captain don Francisco de Ovalle and doña María Pastene, his wife.

    On the same day, José, the legitimate son of don Fernando de Irarrázaval y Zárate and of his wife doña Antonia de Aguilera y Estrada, was anointed with oil and chrism. The child was baptized conditionally at this time. The godparents were the treasury official Antonio de Azoca and his wife doña Isabel Guajardo.*

*The sponsors both descended from conquistadores.

    E.   Baptismal Record of Juan de Irarrázaval y Bravo de Saravia.
        (APS, B, Book IX, f 217v, GL 797291)

Juan, the legitimate son of captain don Fernando Francisco de Irarrázaval and of doña Agustina Bravo de Saravia, was baptized and anointed with oil and chrism on April 17, 1682. The child was eight days old. The godfather was President and Governor don Juan Henríquez.*

*No godmother is named.

F. Baptismal Record of Juana de Toro Mazote y la Serna.
(APS, BMV, Book IV, f 104, GL 797289)

Juana, the infant daughter of Ginés de Toro Mazote and of his legitimate wife doña Elena de la Serna, was baptized on January 19, 1582. The child was anointed with oil and chrism. The godparents were Agustín Briceño and Francisca Tarabajano, his legitimate wife.*

*Francisca was of illegitimate birth but licitly married.

G. Marriage Certificate of Manuel de Toro Mazote and doña Juana de Cifuentes Hidalgo.
(APS, BMV, Book IV, f 101, GL 797289)

On July 5, 1621, I, the Dean don Jerónimo de Agurto officiated at the marriage and the nuptial blessing of the secretary (sic) Manuel de Toro Mazote and doña Juana de Cifuentes Hidalgo. The attendants were Juan de Astorga and his wife doña Beatriz Navarro.

Appendix 2

Royal Revenue Derived from Toro Mazote Proprietary Offices 1584-1674

As the following informal table shows, the Spanish Hapsburgs did not grow wealthy from the money they received from the proprietary public trusteeship and the office of notary and cabildo clerk. The crown's expenses in Chile were heavy. Administrative costs, including the salaries for governors and audiencia ministers, had to be paid. Through the royal military subsidy, the crown sent funds into the colony to support the Araucanian war effort in the seventeenth century. Given the drain on the treasury that Chile represented, the income from the trusteeship and the notarial office appears quite insignificant over the period of ninety years from 1584 to 1674. The colonists who paid the purchase prices, transfer fees, and medianatas quite obviously regarded their investments in public posts as profitable ventures.

The data given in the table are drawn from the Actas cited previously in the text. Only Matias de Toro y Córdoba mentioned the money he spent trying to obtain royal confirmation of the post he lost and regained. Since his assertion cannot be verified and other proprietors kept silent on the subject of expenditures for securing royal confirmation, those costs are not included.

The royal treasury office in Santiago obtained the payments in gold and silver. In the table, abbreviations for the currency are: p = pesos, t = tomines, g = grains, r = reales.

Transfer Fees Paid in Gold:

1584	1,167p	(1/3 of 3,500), notary Ginés de Toro Mazote.
1605	1,500p	notary Ginés de Toro Mazote for depositario Ginés de Toro Mazote y la Serna.
1607	666p, 5t, 4g	notary Manuel de Toro Mazote y la Serna.
Total	3,333p, 5t, 4g	remitted to the royal treasury office in Santiago.

Purchase Prices and Transfer Fees Paid in Silver:

1594	7,600p	in 3 installments, purchase price, depositario Tomás de Olavarría.
1645	2,500p	transfer fee, depositario Pedro de Salinas y Córdoba.
1662	2,333p, 3r	transfer fee, depositario Matías de Toro y Córdoba.
1674	4,500p	in 3 installments, repurchase, depositario Matías de Toro y Córdoba for his son Ginés.
Total	16,933p, 3r	remitted to the royal treasury office in Santiago.

Medianatas Paid in Silver:

1645	125p	Pedro de Salinas y Córdoba
1662	116p, 6r	Matías de Toro y Córdoba
1674	79p, 1r	Matías de Toro y Córdoba
Total	320p, 7r	remitted to the royal treasury office in Santiago.

Appendix 3

Abstracts of Notarial Records
1622-1623

The notarial registry of Manuel de Toro Mazote echoes the tempo and tenor of life in seventeenth-century Santiago. The following abstracts are free translations summarizing powers of attorney, the posting of bond, labor contracts, slave sales, an agreement to settle differences over a slave trade partnership, and a rural land sale. The documents dating from 1622 and 1623 are all located in the Chilean National Archive, in the Archivo de los escribanos de Santiago, vol. 89. Folio numbers are given below. When necessary, explanatory notes are included.

A. Power of Attorney of captain don Diego González Montero to doctor don Pedro Machado, don Florián Girón, and don Gregorio de Castañeda. (fs 180v-181)

Be it known how I, captain don Diego González Montero, vecino encomendero of Indians of the noble and very loyal city of Santiago of the kingdom of Chile empower doctor don Pedro Machado de Chávez, and the maestre de campo (field commander) don Florián

Girón, vecino encomendero of the said city, who are on the way to the court of His Majesty, and captain don Gregorio de Castañeda, my brother-in-law resident at court, together and individually to appear in my name and act for me before the king don Felipe our lord and his royal councils and tribunals and ecclesiastical and secular justices and petition His Majesty, in remuneration of the many services that my parents and forebears and I have performed, to grant me a reward or rewards. They can represent me in civil and criminal cases and take all necessary legal steps. In Santiago, Chile, January 16, 1623, before the clerk of the cabildo. Witnesses Pedro Cortés, the licentiate Juan de Escobar Carrillo, and Antonio de Bocanegra.

Don Diego González Montero

Before me,
Manuel de Toro Mazote
notary public and cabildo clerk
fee: 6 reales

Don Diego, identifying himself as a vecino encomendero and calling attention to his lineage, wanted to bolster his patrician status with royal favors. A copyist wrote the document that Toro Mazote notarized with his signature and official title.

Don Diego's first wife, doña María Clara de Loaisa, had a brother named Gregorio Castañeda. (Roa y Ursúa, 185.)

B. Power of Attorney of Juan García de Valles to his Wife, Mother-in-law, et al. (fs 124-125v)

Be it known how I, Juan García de Valles, vecino of the city of Santiago, Chile execute by the present that I give all my full and sufficient authority as required by law to doña Tomasa Sánchez, my wife, and to Francisca Sánchez, my mother-in-law, and to Juan de León, and to Andrés Barona, and to each one individually in order that in my name they can act for me in all my legal and financial affairs. And if God should be pleased to call me from this life before I make my will, my wife and mother-in-law, but not the others, can make my will. My body is to be interred in a church. I name my legitimate children, all daughters, as my universal heirs and revoke and annul any previous wills, codicils, and powers of attorney that I have made. My wife and mother-in-law can make bequests and legacies as I have informed them to do. In Santiago, Chile, September 28, 1622. Witnesses Nicolás Piñon, Antonio de Bocanegra, Pedro Rosa de Narváez, Gaspar Díaz Hidalgo, and Marcos del Castillo.

Juan García de Valles	Before me, Manuel de Toro Mazote, notary public and cabildo clerk fee: 8 reales.

Juan García de Valles is identified in the ledger, fs 111, 116v-117, as a merchant who was preparing to go to Peru. In his power of attorney, he called himself a vecino in the general sense of the term meaning a resident. A number of Toro Mazote's clients used that loose construction. Francisca Sánchez was not entitled doña, but her son-in-law had enough confidence in her intelligence and good sense to name her along with his wife doña Tomasa to write his will.

C. Power of Attorney of Diego de Morales to captain Luis de Toro. (fs 161-162)

Be it known how I, Diego de Morales y Córdoba, vecino encomendero of Indians of the city of Santiago, Chile, by the present document give all my authority as required by law to captain Luis de Toro Mazote, vecino of this city, in order that in my name he can act for me in all my financial and legal affairs both in and out of court. And I authorize him, if God Our Lord is served to take me from this present life before I have made my will, to make my will for me according to the instructions I have given him. My body is to be interred in the church of Santo Domingo in this city in the tomb that my parents have there. I name him as my executor and my legitimate children as my heirs. I revoke any previous wills and powers of attorney to make my will. Santiago, Chile, November 14, 1622. Witnesses the licentiate Andrés de Toro Mazote, the public trustee Ginés de Toro Mazote, Alonso de Salinas, Diego . . ., and Juan . . .Pajuelo.

Diego de Morales
                      Before me,
                      Manuel de Toro Mazote,
                      notary public and cabildo clerk
                      fee: 8 reales

D. Surety of maestre de campo don Florián Girón for Bernardino de Fuenmayor. (f 123)

In the noble and very loyal city of Santiago, Chile, September 26, 1622, in the presence and with the consent of Ginés de Toro Mazote, depositario general and fiel ejecutor of this city, the maestre de campo don Florián Girón y Montenegro, vecino encomendero of Indians of this city, posts bond for Bernardino de Fuenmayor, master tailor, to underwrite the work of the tailor up to the sum of 500 pesos. Witnesses Antonio de Bocanegra, Inocencio Martínez de Aparicio, and Gaspar Díaz Hidalgo.

Ginés de Toro
don Florián Girón
                      Before me,
                      Manuel de Toro Mazote
                      notary public and cabildo clerk
                      fee: 6 reales

Ginés de Toro Mazote was using his authority as city inspector to approve the bond.

Don Florián, a peninsular, married a relative of doña Marina Ortiz de Gaete. (Roa y Ursúa, 567.)

E. Surety of captain Fuenzalida for Francisco de Miranda in the administration of Rapel and Ligueimo. (f 136)

In the noble and very loyal city of Santiago, Chile on November 12, 1622, with the consent of the protector of the Indians, sergeant major Andrés Jiménez de Lorca, captain Francisco de Fuenzalida becomes the bondsman of Francisco de Miranda regarding the administration of Rapel and Ligueimo. Miranda has been appointed to and received for the office of administrator. The bondsman underwrites Fuenzalida's financial responsibility toward the Indian villages. Witnesses captain don Francisco de Eraso, don Antonio Fernández Caballero, and Antonio de Bocanegra.

Andrés Jiménez de Lorca	Before me,
Francisco de Fuenzalida	Manuel de Toro Mazote
	notary public and
	cabildo clerk
	fee: 6 reales

In contrast to the previous bond, this document mentions no monetary sum. The pueblo of Rapel belonged to the Irarrázaval encomienda. The notary incorrectly dated the surety document 1623, but it is correctly placed between items in November, 1622, while Miranda was the administrator of the two villages. (Actas, XXVIII, 91, records his appointment and reception under the date Nov. 11, 1622.)

F. Contract of Bartolomé, cartwright, with Alonso de Salinas. (f 104)

In the noble and very loyal city of Santiago, Chile, August 19, 1622, before the señor doctor Gaspar de Narváez y Valdelomar of the council of His Majesty and his oidor in the royal audiencia of this kingdom, and before me, the notary, there appeared Bartolomé, an Indian who is a native of Osorno, a cartwright, and Alonso de Salinas, vecino of this city, and they said that they are making a contract and are agreed that, in view of the good treatment that the aforesaid had received in a previous contact, Bartolomé will serve at his trade for one year from today. For each new cart that he makes, with Salinas furnishing the wood, tools, and other things, and food, he is to be paid twelve silver pesos. For those carts that he mends so that they are like new, six, and for those that he fixes up, he will receive what they will agree upon in regard to the amount of work it takes. During the year, he will not be absent. If he should be absent or become ill, he will serve additional time in the future. His Grace approves the contract, because the Indian enters it willingly, insofar as it does not infringe on the rights of a third party. Witnesses don Francisco de Villalobos y Mercado and Gaspar Díaz Hidalgo. And His Grace and the executor, whom I certify that I know, signed their names. Another witness was Diego Navarro.

El doctor Narváez y Valdelomar Alonso de Salinas	Before me, Manuel de Toro Mazote notary public and cabildo clerk fee: 8 reales.

Doctor Narváez y Valdelomar took office as an oidor in Santiago on January 19, 1622. (Silva i Molina, 29-35.) He thus participated in the quarrel between the high court and the city council on the authorization of Indian work contracts.

G. Contract of Alvaro de Vivero with Juan García Mezo. (f 123v)

In the noble and very loyal city of Santiago, Chile, September 26, 1622, before the licentiate Toro, alcalde ordinario of the said city, and before me, the notary, Alvaro de Vivero appeared and said that is his name. He is a youth who appears to be sixteen years old, and he says that he is an orphan and that of his free will he desires to make a contract with Juan García Mezo, master barber, in order that he teach him the said trade for the time of three years from today. During which time, he promises not to be absent, and, if he is absent because of illness, he will serve in future. The aforesaid Juan García Mezo obliged himself to teach the trade, and to provide housing and food and medical expenses if the youth becomes ill. He will also provide clothing, including a suit of clothes, shirts, a hat, shoes, and stockings. If the barber does not teach as he should, the instruction will be furnished by another at his cost. They request His Grace to approve the contract. His Grace, the aforesaid alcalde, approves, provided the contract does not prejudice the rights of a third party. Witnesses Antonio de Bocanegra, Inocencio Martínez de Aparicio, and Martín García. I certify that I know the parties, and they sign their names.

Licentiate Toro	Before me,
Juan Garcia de Mezo	Manuel de Toro Mazote
Alvaro de Vivero	notary public and
	cabildo clerk
	gratis

H. Contract of Fernando, an Indian, with Gaspar, a Tailor. (f 124)

In the noble and very loyal city of Santiago, Chile, September 26, 1622, before the licentiate Toro, alcalde ordinario of the said city, and before me, the notary, Francisco de Espinosa Caracol, a priest--and with the free will of Fernando, an Indian, who says that he is in the service of the ecclesiastic--makes a contract with Gaspar de Agurto, tailor, in order that for the time of two years, he will teach him all that he knows of the trade. Fernando desires to learn and will not be absent, and, if he is, he has to serve in future. For his work he is to have a suit of clothes each year, housing, and food. Moreover, Fernando has to do the tailoring, that he knows how to do, for Francisco de Espinosa Caracol without charging for it. Gaspar de Agurto accepts the contract and agrees to teach Fernando all that he knows. If he does not do so, he can be taught at Agurto's expense. Francisco de Espinosa Caracol will not take the Indian away during the time of the contract, and, if he does so, he will pay damages. At their request, His Grace approves the contract provided that it does prejudice the rights of a third party. Witnesses Antonio de Bocanegra, Martín García, and Gaspar Díaz Hidalgo. His Grace and the licentiate Francisco de Espinosa signed. A witness signed for Agurto.

Licentiate Toro	Before me,
Francisco de Espinosa	Manuel de Toro Mazote
By the witness Antonio de Bocanegra	notary public and cabildo clerk
	Although I requested a fee, they did not give me anything.

Father Espinosa y Caracol was born in Osorno and spent much of his life in the south. (Roa y Ursúa, 241.)

I. Slave Sale by Duarte Gómez to captain Pedro del Portillo for doña Mariana de Villagra. (fs 194-194v)

Be it known how I, Durate Gómez de Miranda, resident in the city of Santiago, Chile, and on my way to the port of Buenos Aires, sell to captain Pedro del Portillo, who is acting for doña Mariana de Villagra, the widow of captain don Juan de Rivadeneira, my two black slaves from Angola, recently come from their homeland, named Inés, about ten years old, and María, about eighteen to twenty years old, free at present of illness. I do not guarantee them to be free of vices or defects because they are bozales, mere skin and bones, and I only assure her that they are captives of a just war, slaves subject to perpetual slavery, and the royal taxes have been paid. The price of 920 pesos is due in 8 months. Captain Pedro del Portillo accepts the terms for the aforesaid. Witnesses Pedro Rosa de Narváez, Juan Rosa de Narváez, and Gaspar Díaz Hidalgo. In the city of Santiago, Chile, February 25, 1623.

Pedro del Portillo
Duarte Gómez de Miranda

Before me,
Manuel de Toro Mazote
notary public and
cabildo clerk
fee: 6 reales

Doña Mariana's parents were Juan de Villagra and doña Mariana Olmos de Aguilera. Her father was related to Governor Francisco de Villagra; her maternal relatives included doña Antonia de Aguilera y Estrada. She was the second wife of Juan de Rivadeneira, the sole heir of "captain" Juan Gómez and doña Francisca de Escobedo. (Espejo, Nobiliario, 42-43, 76-77.)

J. Slave Sale by captain don Fernando Bravo to my lady doña Catalina Justiniano. (fs 191v-192)

Be it known that I, captain don Fernando Bravo de Naveda, resident in this city of Santiago, Chile, and on my way to the port of Buenos Aires, sell to doña Catalina Justiniano--wife of the licentiate Francisco Pastene, who has a power of attorney from her husband to act in this matter, and I, Bravo, have spoken with her husband who is presently ill--my black slave woman named Lucrecia, born in Angola, some fifty years of age, and her children named Domingo, five years old, and Ana, four years old, recently come from their homeland. The three have been in her power and serving her for three months. And I sell them as slaves taken in a just war, subject to perpetual servitude, and free of sales tax (alcabala), and with the royal taxes paid. The woman is sick and has defects. I sell them for the price of 600 pesos that I have received and transfer all my rights to the slaves to the aforesaid. Doña Catalina Justiniano accepts this sale as it is stated and says she has had the blacks in her service for three months. In Santiago, Chile, February 23, 1623. Witnesses Jerónimo López de Ribera, Gaspar Díaz Hidalgo, and Diego Rodrigo (sic). I know the parties and a witness signs for the party who does not know how to write.

Don Fernando Bravo
Diego Rodrigo Guzmán

Before me,
Manuel de Toro Mazote
notary public and cabildo clerk
gratis

Doña Catalina's ancestry included Italians as well as Spaniards. Her father-in-law was a conquistador. (Espejo, Nobiliario, 640.)

K. Slave Sale by captain San Juan de Hermua to don Cristóbal Pizarro. (f 179)

Be it known how I, captain San Juan de Hermua, vecino morador of the city of Santiago, Chile, execute by the present that I sell to don Cristóbal Pizarro my black slave named Domingo, some twenty years of age, from Biafra, who belonged to Pedro de Elguea. Don Cristóbal has had Domingo working for him for over a year and is satisfied with his work and that he does not have any vice or illness. I sell him for the price of 470 pesos that has been paid in hemp, at 17 pesos per hundredweight. Captain Juan Alonso Granada, with a power of attorney from don Cristóbal Pizarro, agrees to the terms. In Santiago, Chile, January 17, 1623. Witnesses Antonio de Bocanegra, notary of His Majesty, captain Juan Antonio de Fuenzalida, and Pedro Rosa de Narváez.

San Juan de Hermua	Before me,
Juan Alonso Granada	Manuel de Toro Mazote
	notary public and
	cabildo clerk
	(no fee mentioned)

A copyist wrote the bill of sale up to the list of witnesses. Toro Mazote finished and notarized the document in his own hand.

L. Slave Sale by Bartolomé de Rojas y Puebla to doña Francisca Pajuelo. (f 163v)

Be it known how I, Bartolomé de Rojas y Puebla, vecino morador of the city of Santiago, Chile, sell to doña Francisca Pajuelo, widow of captain Jerónimo de Molina, my black slave named Sebastián, a native of Angola, recently come from his homeland and mere skin and bones, of some twenty-four years of age, captured in a just war, free of sales tax, without assuring her of anything other than the fact he is a slave and subject to servitude and while he has been in my power he has not had any vice or contagious illness other than a rash. I have received the price of 450 pesos. In Santiago, Chile, December 19, 1622. Witnesses Antonio de Bocanegra, Pedro Rosa de Narváez, and Gaspar Díaz Hidalgo. The executor and the licentiate Molina, who accepted for his mother, signed their names.

Bartolomé de Rojas y Puebla	Before me,
Luis de Molina y Parraguez	Manuel de Toro Mazote
	notary public and
	cabildo clerk
	(no fee mentioned)

Doña Francisca's parents were the conquistador Pero Gómez de Don Benito and doña Isabel Pardo Parraguez. The licentiate Molina was a priest who became a cathedral canon (Roa y Ursúa, 34-35, 351-353.) Jerónimo de Molina was the merchant who led the fight for moradores to become eligible for city council membership.

M. Agreement between Juan Andrés de León and Alonso Bello re a Slave Trade Partnership. (fs 138v-139v)

Be it known how we, Juan Andrés de León and Alonso Bello, vecinos and residents in this city of Santiago, Chile, say that we have accounts in regard to the money that Bello handled when he brought blacks to sell here. To preserve our friendship, we have agreed to settle our differences and the accounts by putting them in the hands of third parties and an arbitrator, and we will abide by the decision reached. I, Juan Andrés de León, name for my part captain Juan Bernardo Jaramillo, and the aforesaid Alonso names the alférez Bartolomé de Rojas y Puebla, who within four days of being informed of this agreement will render their judgment on the matter. In the event that they cannot agree, we name captain Pedro del Portillo as arbitrator. And as accountants to audit the records, León names Nicolás Otavio, and Bello names Esteban Pablo de Ojeda. January 17, 1623. Witnesses Antonio de Bocanegra, captain Luis de Toro Mazote, and Pedro Rosa de Narváez.

Juan Andrés de León
Alonso Bello

Before me,
Manuel de Toro Mazote
notary public and
cabildo clerk
fee: 6 reales

N. Land Sale by captain Jorge de Fernández to the secretary Pedro Valiente. (fs 128-128v)

Be it known how I, captain Jorge Fernández de Aguiar, vecino of the city of Santiago, sell to secretary Pedro Valiente de la Barra 300 <u>cuadras</u> (literally, blocks) of land that I have in the jurisdiction of the city of Concepción of this kingdom. I received title to the land from Governor Alonso de Ribera. I have occupied the land with people, livestock, and crops for four years. (Boundaries are identified by neighboring estancias.) I sell the land and water rights for the price of 250 pesos that I have received from Pedro Valiente de la Barra. Witnesses the licentiate Francisco de Escobar, the licentiate Cristóbal de Escobar, and Pedro Rosa de Narváez.

Jorge Fernández de Aguiar

Before me,
Manuel de Toro Mazote
notary public and
cabildo clerk
fee: 6 reales

Valiente was the official secretary of Governor Pedro Osores de Ulloa. (Roa y Ursúa, 576.)

ABBREVIATIONS

The following abbreviations are used in the notes and bibliography:

APS	Archivo de la parroquia del sagrario Santiago de Chile; cited by Genealogical Library film numbers; acronyms indicate records of baptisms, marriages, velaciones, and confirmations.
BACH	Boletín de la academia chilena de la historia.
BAE	Biblioteca de autores españoles.
BHC	Biblioteca hispano-chilena (Medina).
DIF	Colección de documentos inéditos, 1st ser. (Medina).
DIS	Colección de documentos inéditos, 2nd ser. (Medina).
ES	Chile, Archivo Nacional, Archivo de los escribanos de Santiago.
HAHR	Hispanic American Historical Review.
Historiadores	Colección de historiadores (Medina and others).
RCHG	Revista chilena de historia y geografía.
RLRI	Recopilación de leyes de los reynos de las Indias.
TAm	The Americas: A Quarterly Review of Inter-American Cultural History.

NOTES

(Complete authors' names, titles, and publication data are given in the bibliography.)

Introduction

    1. Mörner, "Economic Factors," 355-369.

    2. Góngora, Encomenderos, passim, and "Social Stratification," 421-448.

    3. Mörner, "Economic Factors," 363-364; Barbier, "Elite," 416-435, and Bourbon Chile, 31-52.

    4. Loveman, 74.

    5. Korth's Spanish Policy parallels the chronological coverage of this present volume.

    6. Flusche and Korth, Forgotten Females, passim, and "Dowry Office"; Korth and Flusche, "Dowry and Inheritance."

    7. Mörner, "Economic Factors," 362.

    8. Lockhart, Peru, 43; Barbier, Bourbon Chile. Amunátegui Solar, Mayorazgos, with its documentary appendices proved particularly helpful not only in selecting the families to study in this book but also in providing basic data on individuals.

Part I: Patricians

    1. As shown in the bibliography, the letters of Cortés and the Bernal Díaz classic are available in English translation, while BAE includes an edition of Valdivia's letters. Américo Castro finds the origins of the conquistador ethos in medieval Spain.

    2. Edwards, 204-205.

    3. Mörner, Race Mixture, 54; he comments on recent criticism of this early view in "Economic Factors," 335-336.

    4. Edwards, 206, 224; Eyzaguirre, 78.

5. Eyzaguirre, 101-116; Ramón Folch, 192 and notes 1-2. The jurist Solórzano y Pereyra noted that the term feudatarios was used in both the law and common language, especially in Peru, to designate encomenderos, but he added that encomiendas differed sharply from true *feudos*. See *Política indiana*, Book III, ch. 3, nos. 27-28.

6. Korth, *passim*.

7. Meza Villalobos, citing many municipal and royal documents, furnishes an instructive view of the aristocratic mentality with emphasis on its political implications across the colonial centuries; the quotations are 20-21, 162, 167. See also *Siete Partidas*, *Partida* II, titles 1-5, 10, 13; *Partida* III, title 18, laws 49-51, for medieval statements on kingship and royal rewards.

8. Painter, 28-64.

9. DIF, XXIII-XXVII, compiles Chilean probanzas, primarily from the sixteenth century, and serves unless otherwise indicated as the basis for the discussion in the text. Selections from northern New Spain in Israel Cavazos Garza may be consulted for comparative purposes.

10. Hanke, 5-10.

11. Examples are found in DIF, XVIII, 435-483.

12. Meza Villalobos, 55-57.

13. Barbier, *Bourbon Chile*, 45-48, and Lohmann Villena, *Audiencia de Lima*, give attention to marital alliances.

Chapter 1

1. Roa y Ursúa, 329-331. Thayer Ojeda, *Familia*, and Silva Castro, drawing heavily on the former's data in *Formación*, II, 161-176, attest to the family's prominence.

2. Bermúdez Plata, III, 210; Roa y Ursúa, 331; Mujica, 21-23; Amunátegui Solar, *Mayorazgos*, I, 271-274; Espejo, *Nobiliario*, 870-872; Silva Castro, 21-22; Thayer Ojeda, *Familia*, 11-43, 209-239. Lockhart, *Peru*, 34-48, 153-154, discusses rank and the use of don and doña.

3. Amunátegui Solar, Mayorazgos, I, 274-275; Mujica, 23-24; Medina, in the appendices to his editon of Ercilla, V, 32. Thayer Ojeda, Familia, 240-241.

4. Amunátegui Solar, Mayorazgos, I, 275; Eyzaguirre, 102; Bermúdez Plata, III, 134, 137-138, 169-170, 184-187; Valdivia to Prince Philip and Charles V, Santiago, Oct. 26, 1552, in Cartas, 69-75; see also data on Alderete in DIF, IX, 244-265, XIII, passim.

5. Bermúdez Plata, III, x-xi, 206-210.

6. "Probanza de los méritos y servicios de don Francisco de Irarrázaval," Lima, Sept., 1559, in DIF, XXIII, 39. Vargas Ugarte, II, 33-52, treats the Hernández Girón rebellion.

7. Roa y Ursúa, 331.

8. Amunátegui Solar, Mayorazgos, I, 274-275, and Princess Juana to the governor of Chile, Valladolid, March 5, 1555, 351; Thayer Ojeda, Familia, 237-239.

9. Eyzaguirre, 76-79; DIF, XIII, passim; Bibar, 197-198; Góngora Marmolejo, 124.

10. Loveman, 52-55, 60-62; Eyzaguirre, 74-82, 90, 107-108.

11. Hanke, 1; Korth, 31-55; Parry and Keith, V, 400-408, 413-416.

12. DIF, XXIII, 39-53; Góngora Marmolejo, 124-141; Mariño de Lobera, 363-413; Bibar, 204; Ercilla, I, Part II, canto 19, octava 48, canto 25, octava 59; Amunátegui Solar, Mayorazgos, I, 276-278.

13. Unless otherwise indicated the analysis in the text is based on "Probanza," in DIF, XXIII, 39-53. RLRI, Book II, title 33, law 1, dating from 1542, empowered audiencias to give permission for informaciones.

14. Mariño de Lobera, 390.

15. Korth, 25. Charges against Governor Hurtado de Mendoza regarding encomienda grants figured prominently in his residencia, see DIF, XXVIII, 377-443.

16. Gibson, 38-43.

17. Korth, 25-50.

18. Viceroy Hurtado de Mendoza to the king, Lima, Oct. 28, 1559, in DIF, XXVIII, 312; Amunátegui Solar, Mayorazgos, I, 279.

19. Amunátegui Solar, Mayorazgos, I, 280, and Royal decree, Toledo, Feb. 19, 1561, 354.

20. Royal decree, Toledo, Jan. 22, 1561, in DIS, I, 18-19. Amunátegui Solar, Mayorazgos, I, 280 and note 1, and in transcribing the decree, 352-353, indicates that Irarrázaval had been promoted to gentilhombre de la boca.

21. Royal decree, Toledo, Jan. 22, 1561, in DIS, I,18-19.

22. Royal decree, Madrid, Nov. 19, 1551, in Documentos . . . de América y Oceanía, XVIII, 16-18.

23. Espejo, Nobiliario, 872, 888; Roa y Ursúa, 331; Schäfer, I, 380; Thayer Ojeda, Familia, 51, 61-64, 241-243; Amunátegui Solar, Mayorazgos I, 280; Francisco Caro de Torres, Historia de las órdenes militares de Santiago, Calatrava y Alcántara desde su fundación hasta el rey don Felipe segundo (1629), quoted in Silva Castro, 33-34. Korth and Flusche treat dowry law in "Dowry and Inheritance." Doña Lorenza was born in Seville but of Basque extraction. See Gibson, 100-101, on the House of Trade.

24. Irarrázaval to the Council of the Indies, Lima, Nov. 10, 1563, in DIF, XXIX, 292-293.

25. Espejo, Nobiliario, 887-890. Lockhart in Peru and Cajamarca and with Enrique Otte in Letters traces the importance of family connections in the process of colonization.

26. Writ of encomienda, Santiago, Sept. 2, 1564, in DIS, I, 17-21, and DIF, XI, 441-444.

27. Roa y Ursúa, 332; Espejo, Nobiliario, 873-874, 891.

28. DIS, I, 17-21; DIF, XI,441-444.

29. DIS, I, 21-23.

30. Ibid., 17-24.

31. Irarrázaval to the king, Lima, Nov. 20, 1564, in DIF, XXIX, 382-384. He reviewed his roles as messenger to and from Chile in a deposition for Pedro de Villagra's probanza in Lima, Dec., 1565, in ibid., 448, 521-531.

32. Ibid., 382-384.

33. An example is Amunátegui Solar, Encomiendas, II, part 2, 14-23.

34. Ots Capdequí summarizes legislation on encomienda inheritance by widows and children, 225-229.

35. DIF, XXIX, 384.

36. Lockhart, Peru, 151, 196-198.

37. DIF, XXIX, 384.

38. Royal decree, Segovia, Aug. 7, 1565, in Amunátegui Solar, Mayorazgos, I, 352-353; see also DIS, I, 99.

39. The discussion of the lawsuits is expanded in the following chapter; Amunátegui Solar, Mayorazgos, I, 282-286, and Encomiendas, II, part 2, 31-41, 60-69, 127, furnishes a useful synopsis of the many-sided litigation.

Chapter 2

1. Court records tracing the encomienda's history are in DIF, XI, 311-556; XXIII, 53-93; Parry and Keith, V, 416-418.

2. DIF, XI, 419-422, XXV, 182-187. The writ of encomienda and act of possession both carry the date Dec. 31, 1561. Hurtado de Mendoza was no longer governor at that time, Eyzaguirre, 82. The seeming discrepancy stems from the sixteenth-century practice of using Christmas as the beginning of the new year. An example is the city council session for Dec. 31, 1566, which is dated 1567, Actas, XVII, 127. See also Vivar, 314 note 1396.

3. DIF, XI, 311-319, 385-549; XXIII, 53-93 items 2-4, 6-10.

4. Ibid., XXIII, 68.

5. Ibid., XI, 425-430, 451-540 item 17; 55-92 items 8-9, 19. An anonymous critic faulted Francisco de Villagra for depriving encomenderos and encomenderas of their grants in order to practice nepotism and favoritism, Historiadores, XXIX, 507-512. Roa y Ursúa, 83-85, 134-135, 149, 371, establishes relationships; Mazo de Alderete was not a member of Governor Alderete's immediate family but may have been a relative.

6. Meza Villalobos, 39-40.

7. DIF, XIII, 484-485.

8. Roa y Ursúa, 41-42; Espejo, Nobiliario, 72-77. Juan Gómez regularly used that simple signature in DIF, XI, which is devoted entirely to cases involving him; others occasionally referred to him as Juan Gómez de Almagro.

9. DIF, XI, 5-229.

10. Ibid., 132.

11. Vivar, 200-208; Góngora Marmolejo, 102-108; Mariño de Lobera, 338-341.

12. DIF, XI, 186-189.

13. Ibid., 5-311. Orense was carrying news of Valdivia's death to Spain; the messages were salvaged from the shipwreck, Vivar, 208; Góngora Marmolejo, 116, 120, 141; Mariño de Lobera, 343; Errázuriz, 383-384; Barros Arana, II, 32-33 and note 7.

14. DIF, XI, 5-229.

15. Ibid., 229-311.

16. Mujica de la Fuente, 312-313.

17. DIF, XI, 229-234. Amunátegui Solar, Encomiendas, I, 66-67, II, part 2, 43-47; Thayer Ojeda, Santiago, 126; Roa y Ursúa, 118, 373, treat Antonio de Tarabajano, his daughter, and her husband. DIF, XV, 217-307, contains Tarabajano's información on services and a suit involving Briceño and the Gualemo encomienda.

18. Mujica de la Fuente, 315; Thayer Ojeda and Larraín, 43; Thayer Ojeda, Formación, II, 54; Medina, in Ercilla, V, 128.

19. <u>DIF</u>, XXIII, 75.
20. Ibid., 53-93.
21. Ibid., items 10-11, 17.
22. Ibid., items 16-18.
23. Ibid.
24. Ibid., items 12-14.
25. Ibid.
26. Ibid.
27. Ibid., XI, 454. See Lockhart, <u>Peru</u>, 34-35, on the widespread use of the term hidalgo.
28. <u>DIF</u>, XI, 446-454, 540-556; XXIII, 56 item 15.
29. Ibid., XI, 511; XXIII, 61-91 item 15.
30. Ibid., XI, 446-540.
31. On the military subsidy (<u>situado</u>) and salaried troops, see Korth, 200, 212-215; Loveman, 59, 71, 73, 93, 111.
32. Documentation on the services of Juan Jufré and Diego Ortiz de Gatica in <u>DIF</u>, XV, 30-31, 465, provides examples.
33. Ibid., XI, 447-540 items 5-9.
34. Ibid., XXIII, 57, 62-92 item 21.
35. Ibid., XI, 452, 458-538 item 19.
36. Ibid., XXIII, 56-57, 62-92 items 16-17, 20.
37. Vega Sarmiento to the king, Lima, incorrectly dated February 1, 1561, in <u>DIF</u>, XXIX, 98-99. The letter refers to the creation of the audiencia of Concepción. The decrees instituting the high court date from 1563, and it began to function in 1567, Schäfer, II, 516; Eyzaguirre, 98. Roa y Ursúa, 310-311, mentions Vega Sarmiento's voluminous correspondence.
38. Irarrázaval to the king, Lima, Feb. 1, 1566, in <u>DIS</u>, I, 57-59.

39. The Santiago city council appointed Gómez procurator for the city and empowered him to act before the king and the pope on Sept. 15, 1564; the power of attorney appears in DIF, XXV, 205-208; see also Mujica de la Fuente, 312. Ercilla, I, Part I, canto 4, treats Gómez and the relief column. Regarding his certification of La Araucana, see ibid., IV, 4-5, 72.

40. DIS, I, 99; Amunátegui Solar, Mayorazgos, I, 286, Encomiendas, II, part 2, 68-69; Mujica de la Fuente, 312-316; Thayer Ojeda, Formación, II, 54, 169; Medina, Diccionario, 358-359. Gómez died in Panamá by 1569.

Chapter 3

1. Amunátegui Solar, Mayorazgos, I, 287-295, is a helpful outline of don Francisco's career after he became a Chilean resident. See also Thayer Ojeda, Formación, II, 169-174, and Familia, 55-60.

2. Roa y Ursúa, 332.

3. DIF, XXIX, 382-384; DIS, I, 57-59. Quiroga, the husband of doña Inés Suárez, was an original conquistador entrusted with the interim governorship on several occasions and appointed governor by the crown in the 1570s, Roa y Ursúa, 38-39. While Costilla was in Chile, Irarrázaval was in Charcas, DIF, XXIX, 528.

4. DIS, I, 100-103; Espejo, Nobiliario, 42, 178-181, 793-794, 874-878, 890.

5. DIS, I, 97-99.

6. Góngora, Encomenderos, 135-136.

7. Roa y Ursúa, 332.

8. Eyzaguirre, 113-139; Colección de documentos inéditos para la historia de Hispano-América, III, 211.

9. DIS, I, 110-111; Cano Roldán, 98-105.

10. Cano Roldán, 109-120.

11. Thayer Ojeda, Familia, 103-107; Roa y Ursúa, 248-250, 293-294; DIS, I, 175-193.

12. Espejo, <u>Nobiliario</u>, 42-43, 178-181, 874-878; <u>DIS</u>, I, 306-316, 413-416; Roa y Ursúa, 404.

13. Góngora, "Cuentas," 33, 35, 36, 43; Thayer Ojeda, <u>Santiago</u>, 64, 148.

14. Lillo, <u>Mensuras</u>, II, 185-189; Espejo, <u>Nobiliario</u>, 40-43; Korth and Flusche, 397, mention the legal capacity of widows.

15. Espejo, <u>Nobiliario</u>, 874.

16. Thayer Ojeda, <u>Santiago</u>, 64; <u>Actas</u>, XVII, 345 (1574: July 20); Espejo, <u>Nobiliario</u>, 888-890. On Toledo's tour of the Andean regions, see Vargas Ugarte, II, 236-239.

17. Góngora Marmolejo, 221; <u>Actas</u>, XVII, 362-373 (1575: Jan. 26); Lafuente Machain, 474-476; Schäfer, II, 125-126, 547; Parry and Keith, V, 316-322; Medina, in Ercilla, V, 35 and note 21. Juan Ortiz de Zárate was both governor and <u>adelantado</u>.

18. Góngora, "Social Stratification," 43; Roa y Ursúa, 332; <u>Actas</u>, XVII, 479-511 (1577); XVIII, 1-2, 268, 286-287 (1578: Jan. 1; 1581: Jan. 1, April 13, 21); XIX, 174, 182 (1584: Jan. 1, 14) ; XX, 639-641 (1584 [sic] : Jan. 3-Jan. 18).

19. Ibid., XVIII, 254, 286-287 (1580: Nov. 11; 1581: April 13, 21).

20. Korth, 68-71.

21. <u>Actas</u>, XVIII, 230, 233-245, 258-259 (1581: Sept. 20, 24, Dec.9).

22. Ibid., XVIII, 342 (1581: Nov. 21); XIX, 29-30, 48-50 (1582: May 26, Oct. 12). Vargas Ugarte, II, 284-286, treats the Lima provincial council.

23. <u>Actas</u>, XIX, 50-52 (1582: Oct. 12). The Inquisitors issued the letter of appointment in Lima on Jan. 30, 1582. See Kamen, 147-149, and Flusche, "Councilmen and the Church," 185-186, on familiares; Medina, <u>Inquisición</u>, I, compiles data on early cases in Chile; Ramón Folch, 192 note 2, states that the office of familiar was a mark of honor.

24. Lillo, II, 311-312.

25. Actas, I, 124 (1547: May 2), the cabildo authorized the use of the 25-foot vara. For measuring cloth, the vara equivalent to approximately one yard remained in force.

26. Lillo, II, 311-313.

27. Ibid., 313-316.

28. Roa y Ursúa, 458.

29. Actas, XVIII, 286-287 (1581: April 13, 21).

30. Eyzaguirre, 84; Espejo, Nobiliario, 754; DIS, VI, 343-349.

31. Korth, 70-73.

32. Amunátegui Solar, Mayorazgos, I, 292; Thayer Ojeda, Familia, 60.

33. APS (GL 797288), BMVC, Book I, f 11v; the child's godparents were Luis, a black man, and Beatriz, a black slave.

34. Mendiburu, XI, 371; Espejo, Nobiliario, 873; Thayer Ojeda, Familia, 58-59 and note 13.

35. Mujica, 25-26; Espejo, Nobiliaro, 793-794, 872-874; Roa y Ursúa, 331-334; Schäfer, II, 125-126, 516, 517, 547; Amunátegui Solar, Mayorazgos, I, 293-294, 298-299, 301, 302, 308-309, 354-355; Lafuente Machain, 654-655; BHC, I, 299; Thayer Ojeda, Familia, 65, 67-77. As was common, the children elected various surnames from the Irarrázaval y Zárate family tree.

36. Espejo, Nobiliario, 230-231, 873, 888-889, 891; Thayer Ojeda,Familia, 65-66; Amunátegui Solar, Mayorazgos, I, 298-300; APS (GL 797289), BMV, Book II, fs 161, 167v.

37. APS (GL 797289), BMV, Book III, f 158; Medina, Diccionario, 837-838; Amunátegui Solar, Mayorazgos, I, 240-243, 294 note 1, and Encomiendas, I, 278, II, part 2, 78-83; DIS, III, 262-268; Espejo, Nobiliario, 178-181, 876-878.

38. Konetzke, I, 486-487, 542-543. Marital alliances are studied in Lohmann Villena, Audiencia de Lima, and Burkholder and Chandler.

39. Schäfer, II, 125-126 and notes 193-198, 506, 547; DIS, II, 341-345, 468-469.

40. Barros Arana, III, 394 and note 2; Amunátegui Solar, Encomiendas, I, 278, and Mayorazgos, I, 294-295.

41. DIS, IV, is devoted largely to endorsements and criticisms of Sotomayor, see especially 28-57, 121-123, 164-187.

42. Schäfer, I, 206-208 and note 4, II, 467, 530, 557; Caro de Torres, Sotomayor, 3-4, 50-80; Andrews, Last Voyage, 201-203, and Privateering, 179-180; DIS, VI, 343-349.

43. Sotomayor and doña Isabel de Zárate had three children: don Alonso, baptized in 1591 in Santiago with don Ramiriáñez Bravo de Saravia and doña Isabel Osorio de Cáceres as his sponsors; don Carlos, who became a knight of the Order of Santiago; and doña Lorenza, whose two brothers predeceased her. Since she had no heirs, she gave her title to her Irarrázaval relatives in Spain. Roa y Ursúa, 483-484; Espejo, Nobiliario, 754, 875; Lohmann Villena, Americanos, I, 402; Amunátegui Solar, Mayorazgos, I, 309 and note 3; APS (GL 797289), BMV, Book III, f113.

44. Lillo, II, 310, 316-317.

45. Ibid., 310-321. Flusche and Korth, Forgotten Females, 31, 51-57, note the alienation of Indian lands.

46. Góngora, Encomenderos, 19-21.

47. Lillo, I, 64-65, 67-73; Jara, El salario, 50, 52 note 6, 84-85. Leyes de Toro, laws 54-59, refer to authorization from the husband or the courts for a wife to take legal steps; see also Korth and Flusche, 397.

48. Jara, El salario, 47-49, 84-85.

49. Amunátegui Solar, Mayorazgos, I, 293-295; Caro de Torres, Ordenes, quoted in BHC, I, 299.

50. Thayer Ojeda, Familia, 254-257. On tutors and guardians, see Visigothic Code, Book IV, title 2, law 13, title 3, laws 1-4; Partidas, Partida VI, titles

16-19; Fuero real, Book III, title 7, law 3.

51. Korth and Flusche, 395-400.

52. Thayer Ojeda, Familia, 251. Fuero real, Book III, title 5, law 6; Leyes de Toro, laws 31-39, treat wills by proxies.

53. Amunátegui Solar, Mayorazgos, I, 295-296; Thayer Ojeda, Familia, 79; Flusche and Korth, Forgotten Females, 48.

54. Jara, El salario, 54-55, and "Fuentes," IV, 163.

55. Thayer Ojeda, Santiago, 64, 91.

56. Thayer Ojeda, Formación, II, 174-175; Andrews, Last Voyage, 179-234, and Drake's Voyages, 174-177. Drake died of dysentery on this final expedition to the Americas.

57. Caro de Torres, Sotomayor, 66.

58. Ibid., 79-80. The book was first published in 1620, Espejo, Nobiliario, 754 note 3; BHC, I, 167-171.

59. Caro de Torres, Sotomayor, 72-73.

60. Espejo, Nobiliario, 888; Amunátegui Solar, Mayorazgos, I, 298 and note 1.

61. Amunátegui Solar, Mayorazgos, I, 296-297, 300-306; Roa y Ursúa, 333; Silva Castro, 37-38; Flusche and Korth, Forgotten Females, 48; Thayer Ojeda, Familia, 82, 87.

62. DIS, I, 271-281, 306-316, 356-363, 402-410, 434-438; Lillo, II, 185-189; Barros Arana, II, 322 note 30; Espejo, Nobiliario, 41-43, 180-181, 874; Roa y Ursúa, 233-235, 404; Thayer Ojeda, Familia, 82-87, and Formación, II, 175-176, 357-359; Amunátegui Solar, Mayorazgos, I, 304-305, and Encomiendas, II, part 2, 124-125. Doña Antonia de Aguilera y Estrada was a first cousin to doña Inés de Córdoba y Aguilera, the wife of Governor Alonso de Ribera.

63. DIF, XXV, 29-36 and note 1, 180-219; Espejo, Nobiliario, 874-879; Thayer Ojeda, Familia, 88.

Part II: Social Climbers

1. Meza Villalobos, 101, 103.

2. Unless otherwise indicated Góngora, Encomenderos, and "Social Stratification," 421-448, and Meza Villalobos provide the data for these introductory remarks. To go beyond their findings required extensive genealogical research to obtain information on lineage and marriage and intensive study of such primary materials as the Actas of the Santiago cabildo.

3. Lockhart, Peru, 36-37, discusses the Peruvian use of "doña."

4. Actas, XXVIII, 74-77, 195-199 (1622: Oct. 8; 1624: July 14); XXXIII, 249-251 (1647: Dec. 6). Several legal and quasi-legal devices, including dejaciones, were utilized to keep an encomienda within a family.

5. DIS, II, 166-167; Actas, XVII, 29-30 (1558: June 28). See also RLRI, book IV, title 10, law 10; Góngora, Encomenderos, 71. See Lockhart, Peru, 21, on the meaning of casa poblada.

6. DIS, II, 165-167, reproduces the 1554 decree and the audiencia rulings. On Molina and his efforts, see also Góngora, Encomenderos, 71-72.

7. Ibid.; Meza Villalobos, 58; Actas, XVII, 399-400, 413-414, 417-420, 471-482 (1575-1577 sessions). Councilmen used the terms moradores and ciudadanos interchangeably in the sixteenth and early seventeenth centuries.

8. Ibid., XXVIII, 115-116 (1623: Jan. 27); XXXII, 6, 155 (1640: Jan. 4; 1642: Jan. 2); XLII, 280-282 (1690: Feb. 26); Góngora, Encomenderos, 72-75.

9. Actas, I, 192-196, 262-263 (1549: July 26; 1550: Dec. 16); XXV, 183-184 (1617: April 3); XXXI, 205-206 (1636: Oct. 31); XXXIII, 105-108, 181, 249-261 (1646: May 24; 1647: March 27, Dec. 6); XXXIV, 338-341, 363-364 (1653: May 23, Oct. 30); XXXVII, 94-

95 (1665: Dec. 31); XXXVIII, 320-322 (1674: April 21, 25); XLIII, 254-258, 429 (1695: May 6; 1696: Dec. 14); Góngora, Encomenderos, 75-77; Flusche, "Export Policies," 479-498. After 1597 Santiago encomenderos had a general exemption from being called up for military service in the Araucanian war, Actas, XXXI, 410-412 (1639: Nov. 11); Meza Villalobos 116-141.

    10. Góngora, Encomenderos, 72-77; Meza Villalobos, 103.

    11. Góngora, Encomenderos, 74-87, 94-102; Ramón Folch, 192, 195. On vendible office see Parry; Haring, 165-167; and RLRI, book VIII, titles 20-22.

Chapter 4

    1. Thayer Ojeda, Santiago, 165-169, Formación, II, 130, III, 226; Thayer Ojeda and Larraín, 54; Roa y Ursúa, 217, 313.

    2. Góngora, Encomenderos, 73, "Cuentas," 28-37, 41-42; Ramón Folch, 197.

    3. Góngora, Encomenderos, 87-90, 225.

    4. Thayer Ojeda, Santiago, 48, 54, 56, 71, 84, 107; Lillo, II, 205-227.

    5. Góngora, Encomenderos, 71-73; Actas, XX, 236-237 (1590: Jan. 1).

    6. Larraín, "Diego García de Cáceres," 31-113; Thayer Ojeda, Santiago, 129, 165-169, and Formación, II, 41-42, 155-156; Roa y Ursúa, 207, 401. Ramón Folch, 201, classifies doña Elena as an "española no hidalga" and places her husband in the middle-level range.

    7. References to Martínez and the Colina encomienda include Valdivia, 22; Mariño de Lobera, 285; Amunátegui Solar, Encomiendas, II, 115-120; Roa y Ursúa, 137-138, 401; Lockhart, Cajamarca, 304-305; Thayer Ojeda, Formación, 257-258; Larraín, "Colina," 52-90.

8. Amunátegui Solar, <u>Mayorazgos</u>, I, 183-184.

9. Góngora, "Cuentas," 35-36.

10. Amunátegui Solar, <u>Mayorazgos</u>, I, 184; Roa y Ursúa, 401.

11. Korth and Flusche, 398-400, 403-407, treat estate division.

12. Amunátegui Solar, <u>Mayorazgos</u>, I, 188; Roa y Ursúa, 401-402; Thayer Ojeda, <u>Santiago</u>, 226-227; APS (GL 797289), BMV, Book III, fs 106v, 161v. Doña Elena de la Serna was Juan's godmother. The same registry, fs 108, 120v, 140v, 153, 162, 166v, 172, 185, 188, contains the baptismal records for the following legitimate Toro Mazote y la Serna children: Juana, 1582; Miguel Jerónimo, 1583; María Magdalena, 1584; Luis, 1585; Francisco, 15?; Luciana, 1590; Juan, 1592; Teresa, March, 1593; Domingo, Aug., 1593. Godparents included the married couples Agustín Briceño and Francisca Tarabajano, Alonso del Campo Lantadilla and doña Mariana Navarro, and Gaspar de la Barrera and doña Luciana de Vergara. The fact that the last couple were godparents for both Miguel Jerónimo and Luis lends a certain support to the relationship between Ginés de Toro Mazote and Francisco Martínez because doña Luciana was the natural daughter of the latter and María González Cabezudo, see Thayer Ojeda, <u>Santiago</u>, 181-182; Larraín, "Colina," 52-57.

13. Amunátegui Solar, <u>Mayorazgos</u>, I, 184-185; 187-188; <u>Actas</u>, XIX, 239-245 (1585: Jan. 25, Feb. 1); XX, 57-60, 199, 263 (1586: Nov. 14; 1589: Jan. 27; 1590: May 4); XXI, 327, 349 (1606: May 26, Oct. 2); XXIV, 20-22 (1607: April 7). The title to the office from Governor Sotomayor does not refer to Ginés as a don or an hidalgo but states that he is qualified for the post. On the sale of notarial offices, see also <u>RLRI</u>, book VIII, title 21; Parry, 12-20, 62-63.

14. Ramón Folch, 195, 199, 200-201.

15. On the roles and importance of notaries, see Lockhart, <u>Peru</u>, 68-72; Larraín de Castro, 59-60.

16. Amunátegui Solar, Mayorazgos, I, 185-186;
Thayer Ojeda, Santiago, 100-101; Actas, XIX, 245
(1585: Feb. 1); XX, 33-34 (1586: July 8).

17. Thayer Ojeda, Santiago, 53, 57, 100, 106.

18. Lillo, I, 93-96, II, 321-344; Actas, XX, 333
(1591: Oct. 19).

19. Amunátegui Solar, Mayorazgos, I, 188.

20. Góngora, Encomenderos, 48, 73-74; Ramón Folch,
199, 218.

21. Roa y Ursúa, 44-45, 47-49, 152-153, 214-216,
286-288, 401-402, 491; Espejo, Nobiliario, 194-195,
278-279; Thayer Ojeda, Santiago, 226-227; Ramón Folch,
202 note 1.

Chapter 5

1. Amunátegui Solar, Mayorazgos, I, 186-198.

2. Ibid., 190; Roa y Ursúa, 152-153, 214-216,
286-288, 401, 533; Espejo, Nobiliario, 656; Actas,
XXX, 408, 446-451 (1633: March 15, Sept. 16); ES,
LXXXIX, fs 190-191v; Flusche and Korth, Forgotten
Females, 22; APS (GL 797288), BMVC, Book II, f 12v;
(GL 797289), BMV, Book III, f 162, BMV, Book IV, f
104. Doña Juana's brother and sister-in-law, the
licentiate Andrés de Toro Mazote and doña Luisa de
Celada, were witnesses for the nuptial blessing in San
Saturnino on Feb. 14, 1624. The bride who was
baptized as an infant in Jan., 1582, was therefore
forty-two years old. Her son don Fernando was
baptized in 1633; her daughter doña Antonia was the
second wife of Bartolomé Maldonado, the proprietary
secretary of the audiencia.

3. Actas, XX, 540-555, 587-619 (1593: Nov. 5;
1594: July 28); XXI, 234-241 (1605: Sept. 9, 21); L,
xix; Amunátegui Solar, Mayorazgos, I, 189-190; Roa y
Ursúa, 401, 493-494; RLRI, Book VIII, title XX, law 5;
Olavarría took office as protector general of the
Indians of Santiago in 1594, see Jara, "Fuentes," IV,

161-162.

4. Actas, XIX, 239-244 (1585: Jan. 25); XXI, 234-241 (1605: Sept. 9); XXV, 23-24, 75-77, 338-341 (1614: March 22, Dec. 12; 1619: June 3, 28); XXXVI, 133-161 (1662: Dec. 15); XXXVIII, 352-383 (1674: Dec. 24); L, 1; Parry, 19-20; Amunátegui Solar, Mayorazgos, I, 186-187; Góngora, Encomenderos, 96.

5. Amunátegui Solar, Mayorazgos, I, 187 note 4; Góngora, Encomenderos, 169; Actas, XXVIII, 88-90 (1622: Nov. 11); Flusche "Export Policies," passim.

6. Actas, XXV, passim (1614-1615 sessions); XXVIII, 67 (1622: Aug 26); ES, LXXXIX, fs 116, 123.

7. Actas, XXX, 175-179, 185-187, 190, 222-224 (1630: July 29, Aug. 3, 15, Oct. 7); Góngora, Encomenderos, 74-75.

8. Actas, XXX, 408, 451 (1633: March 15, Sept. 16); XXXI, 31, 118-119, 159, 214, 234-238 (1634: Aug. 5; 1635: Aug. 17; 1636: Jan. 4; 1637: Jan 1, April 2); see also Carvallo Goyeneche, II, 471, 474; Bravo de Naveda was replaced as corregidor in April, 1637.

9. Roa y Ursúa, 44-45, 47-49, 402; Concha, 22-23; Espejo, Nobiliario, 277-279, 581; Thayer Ojeda, Santiago, 136-137, 219; Thayer Ojeda and Larraín, 38-39, 54; Amunátegui Solar, Mayorazgos, I, 193-194. Doña Inés was the daughter of Alonso de Córdoba, the Second, and doña Mariana de Morales.

10. Actas, XXXIII, 6-7, 17, 49-52, 67-71, 74-75 (1645: Jan. 24, March 21, Aug. 28, Nov. 24, Dec. 11); XXXVI, 133-161 (1662: Dec. 15); XXXVIII, 362-363 (1674: Dec. 24); Góngora, Encomenderos, 153; APS (GL 797288), BMVC, Book II, f 185. The witnesses for the Salinas y Córdoba-Toro y Celada wedding were don Luis de las Cuevas y Morales and his wife doña Sebastiana de Villanueva. The bridegroom and the best man were first cousins, see Espejo, Nobiliario, 279-281; Thayer Ojeda, Santiago, 190-191, 219. Don Matías no doubt

owed his right to title himself don more to his mother and the relaxation of the rules regarding its use than to his father. The Actas regularly abbreviate media anata.

11. Actas, XXXVIII, 352-383 (1674: Dec. 24).

12. Ibid., XLII, 288 (1687: Sept. 19); XLIII,255-257 (1695: May 6); XLIV, 119-120 (1697: Dec. 14); L, xix, 1; Roa y Ursúa, 401-402; Amunátegui Solar, Mayorazgos, I, 194; Flusche, "Export Policies," 495 note 1, 496.

13. Actas, XXIV, 360-364 (1613: Jan. 1); XXV, 276-281 (1618: July 24); XXVIII, 36-42 (1622: May 20); XXXVIII, 126, 166-167, 169-171, 173 (1671: March-Aug.); XLI, 264 (1683: Dec. 24); XLIII, 178-192 (1694: Aug. 13); Amunátegui Solar, Mayorazgos, I, 193-194; Roa y Ursúa, 551. Data on the marriage of don Matías and doña Beatriz and the baptism of their eleven-month-old son, Juan de Toro Mazote y Eraso, are given in APS (GL 774553), BM, Book 00 (sic), f 11v; (GL 797291), B, Book IX, f 70.

14. Medina, Diccionario, 252-253; Roa y Ursúa, 43, 399-402, 551; Góngora, Encomenderos, 77-81, 96-97, 146; Actas, XXXIV, 363-364 (1653: Oct. 30); Espejo, Cuyo, I, 134-137.

15. Góngora, Encomenderos, 152-153; Espejo, Cuyo, II, 417; Roa y Ursúa, 402, 597-599, 773-774. Apolinarda married Florián Ramírez y Sierra, the son of Agustín de Montalbán y Sierra and doña Luisa de Miranda Jofré; she and Matías had a brother named Luis who was baptized on Sept. 9, 1633, see APS (GL 774553), BM, Book 00, f 5; (GL 797288), BMVC, Book II, f 12.

16. Roa y Ursúa, 597-598; Silva i Molina, 20-21; Schäfer, II, 87-88 and note 75.

17. Amunátegui Solar, Mayorazgos, I, 186, 191-193.

18. Ibid.; Silva i Molina, 20-21; Góngora, Encomenderos, 152, 169; Roa y Ursúa, 57-60, 110-114,

401-402; Espejo, Nobiliario, 45-47; Thayer Ojeda, "Aguirre," 5-43, and Formación, I, 21-65; Larraín, "Riberos," 105-140; Actas, XXV, 70-74, 269-276 (1614: Dec. 9; 1618: July 18); APS (GL 797289), BMV, Book III, f 225v. The conquistador Francisco de Riberos married a niece of doña Marina Ortiz de Gaete, the wife of Pedro de Valdivia.

19. Roa y Ursúa, 401-402, 597-598; Espejo, Nobiliario, 248-249; Amunátegui Solar, Mayorazgos, I, 130-137, 192-193; Silva i Molina, 20-21; Actas, XXVIII, 204-209 (1624: Aug. 21); APS (GL 774548), BM, Book 0, f 29; (GL 797288), BMVC, Book II, fs 22v, 24, 185; (GL 797289), BMV, Book III, fs 225v, 235v, 247, Book IV, fs 26, 37, 63v; (GL 797291), B, Book IX, f 1.

20. Actas, XXIV, 326-332 (1612: May 31); XXV, 53 (1614: Aug. 29); Amunátegui Solar, Mayorazgos, I, 191.

21. Actas, XXV, 70-74, 80-81, 92-93, 108-109, 151, 224, 241, 245, 269-276, 337-338 (1614-1619 sessions); XXVIII, 77-82 (1622: Oct. 8-14).

22. Andrés de Toro Mazote was probably the interim fiscal between Nov., 1620, and Jan., 1622, Amunátegui Solar, Mayorazgos, I, 192; Actas, XXV, 435-441 (1621: Jan. 15); Silva i Molina, 28, 38.

23. Actas, XXXI, 205-206 (1636: Oct. 31).

24. Góngora, Encomenderos, 143, 166, 205-207; Roa y Ursúa, 45-46.

Chapter 6

1. Actas, XXIV, 20-22 (1607: April 7), reproduces the formal renunciation in Manuel's favor dated Aug. 8, 1606.

2. Ibid., 17-28 (1607: April 7); Thayer Ojeda, Santiago, 165, 167, 226-227.

3. Actas, XXIV, 358-359 (1612: Dec. 29); XXXVI, 127 (1661: Nov. 3); Amunátegui Solar, Mayorazgos, I, 198.

4. Góngora, Encomenderos, 168-169, 218-219, 226; Amunátegui Solar, Mayorazgos, I, 198-201; Actas, XXX, 408, 476 (1633: March 15, Dec. 30); XXXI, 7-8 (1634: Jan. 27); APS (GL 797290), BM, Book V, f 11.

5. Actas, XXXIII, 188-190 (1647: June report inserted between meetings).

6. Góngora, Encomenderos, 168-169, 222; Actas, XXXIII, 190-310 (1647-1648 sessions); Flusche, "Councilmen and the Church," 178, "Public Health," 180, "Export Policies," 492.

7. Amunátegui Solar, Mayorazgos, I, 188; Actas, XXIV, 452-453 (1613: Dec. 20); XXV, 7, 67, 80, 127, 169, 239 (1614-1618 sessions); XXX, 86-87 (1629: March 14); XXXI, 90, 248 (1635: March 20, Oct. 28); XXXIV, 68-69 (1650: Nov. 26).

8. Ibid., XXV, 364, 429, 447, 529 (1620: Jan. 3; 1621: Jan. 4, 18, Dec. 14); XXVIII, 47, 61, 65-73, 117, 175-176 (1622: June 28, Aug. 19, Aug. 23-Oct. 3; 1623: Feb. 3; 1624: Jan. 12, 19); XXXI, 70, 94 (1635: Jan. 5, April 13).

9. Data on doña Juana and her family, including her maternal relatives who were directors (mayordomos) of the local hospital, are found in Roa y Ursúa, 207, 402, 477; Espejo, Nobiliario, 194-195; Góngora, "Cuentas," 28-29, 31, 44 note 5; Thayer Ojeda, Santiago, 135, 142; Amunátegui Solar, Mayorazgos, I, 200; Laval, Hospital, passim, and Médicos, 31; APS (GL 797289), BMV, Book IV, f 101.

10. Vázquez de Espinosa, 728-735; Mellafe, Introducción, 226; Loveman, 76; Korth, 224; Barros Arana, IV, 226-227 and note 3; Cano Roldán, 546-552, 556-558. Flusche and Korth, Forgotten Females, 28-32, 58-63, outline roles of working women.

11. Ovalle and Rosales were outstanding seventeenth-century chroniclers. Korth, 84 ff, gives a thorough, cogent analysis of the issues and policies adopted.

12. Ibid.; Loveman, 59, 64-66, 70-71, 78; Actas, XXV, 468 (1621: March 4); XXVIII, 138-140 (1623: April 21); "Tasa de Esquilache," in BHC, I, 134-151.

13. Actas, XXIV-XXV, XXVIII, passim (1611-1623).

14. Meza Villalobos, 39-43, 76.

15. Actas, XXVIII, 6, 8, 43-46 (1622: Jan. 7, 28, June 10, 13, 28).

16. Ibid., 22, 67, 72, 84-85, 91 (1622: April-Oct.).

17. Ibid., XXV, 411-416 (1620: Dec. 13); Góngora, "Documentos," part 2, 151-166.

18. Silva i Molina, Oidores, 22-27; Amunátegui Solar, Personajes, 97-99; Schäfer, II, 446-488, 517; Lohmann Villena, Audiencia de Lima, 163-164; Roa y Ursúa, 616.

19. Barros Arana, IV, 159-180 and note 20; Espejo, Nobiliario, 253-254, 805.

20. Actas, XXV, 416-418, 435-441 ff (1620: Dec. 14; 1621: Jan. 15, and subsequent sessions). Ureta is often identified as a visitador because he held a commission to audit the treasury accounts in Santiago, Roa y Ursúa, 535.

21. Actas, XXV, 487, 497, 524 (1621: June 4, Aug. 11, Nov. 19); XXVIII, 27-34, 121, 131-133, 141 (1623: Feb. 25, March 4, April 28); XXXI, 175, 192-193, 205 (1636: July 7, Sept. 30, Oct. 31); Roa y Ursúa, 597-598; Espejo, Nobiliario, 619-621.

22. Korth, 114-116; Actas, XXVIII, 86 (1622: Nov. 2); BHC, I, 151-167; Góngora, "Documentos," 166-176. The crown's most complete statement on the Chilean Indians compiling and modifying legislation from the 1620s is RLRI, Book VI, title 16.

23. Actas, XXV, XXVIII, passim (1620-1623 sessions). Lawrence W. Flusche, my father, suggested that a barbecue at the construction site might account for the disappearance of the oxen.

24. <u>Actas</u>, XXV, 463, 489, 516 (1621: March 2, June 26, Oct. 22); XXVIII, 72 (1622: Sept. 16).

25. Ibid., XXV, XXVIII, <u>passim</u> (1620-1623 sessions); Flusche, "Councilmen and the Church," 184.

26. <u>Actas</u>, XXVIII, 47, 95, 99-107 (1622: June 28, Dec. 9, 16, 17).

27. Ibid., XXV, XXVIII, <u>passim</u> (1620-1623 sessions); Flusche, "Public Health," 173-190, "Export Policies," 485, "Councilmen and the Church," 177.

28. Documents in ES, LXXXIX, XCIII, are typical. The cabildo sessions the notary recorded appear in <u>Actas</u>, XXIV-XXV, XXVIII, XXX-XXXVI. See Góngora, "Social Stratification," 428-429, <u>Encomenderos</u>, 98-102, on militia commissions.

29. Unless otherwise indicated, the data discussed in the inventory are found in ES, LXXXIX, fs 97-194v. Each entry in the ledger bears a heading; this facilitates the location of items.

30. Espejo, <u>Nobiliario</u>, 689.

31. Ibid., 619-621; Silva i Molina, 28-29, 40; Schäfer, II, 517, 519.

32. Espejo, <u>Nobiliario</u>, 38-39, 438-439; Amunátegui Solar, <u>Mayorazgos</u>, II, 396-400; Góngora, <u>Encomenderos</u>, 147-148.

33. Espejo, <u>Nobiliario</u>, 665, 724; Góngora, <u>Encomenderos</u>, 77-79, 83-87; <u>Actas</u>, XXVIII, 14-22 (1622: April 7). Jiménez de Lorca left office in 1624, see ibid., 195-199 (1624: July 14).

34. Gubernatorial appointments of corregidores and administrators include <u>Actas</u>, XXVIII, 51-57, 59, 83-84, 91, 110-114 (1622-1623 sessions).

35. Ibid., XXVIII, 51, 67, 73, 88-90 (1622: July 29, Aug. 26, Oct. 7, Nov. 11). As previously explained, the councilmen rotated the staff of office of fiel ejecutor in order to enforce regulations on local businesses.

36. Cédulas dated Dec. 10, 1618 and June 14, 1621, concerning the <u>composición</u> of aliens are in Amunátegui, <u>Precursores</u>, I, 277-281.

37. Roa y Ursúa, 207, 217, 313, 477; Thayer Ojeda, Santiago, 165. Gaspar Hernández de la Serna married Ana Félix de Cifuentes, Juana de Cifuentes Hidalgo's aunt.

38. Actas, XXVIII, 100-104 (1622: Dec. 17); Roa y Ursúa, 427. Toledo y Arbildo had paid his debt in full by July 14, 1623, according to the receipt Toro Mazote appended to the original promissory note.

39. As noted previously, one reason for the shortage of cash was the city council's expenditures on lobbying, see Actas, XXVIII, 135-136 (1623: April 4).

40. Thayer Ojeda, Santiago, 115.

41. The abbess doña Ana María Jófre de Loaysa and the syndic Francisco Alvarez de Toledo both signed the notarized transfer.

42. The novices were doña Ana María de Valenzuela and her sister doña Mencía de Moraga. See also Thayer Ojeda, Santiago, 238; Roa y Ursúa, 174, 177-178.

43. Thayer Ojeda, Santiago, 58-59, 146, 212, 227; Roa y Ursúa, 295, provide data on the persons involved in this case. Doña Luisa de Torres, the mother of the nuns, was the illegitimate daughter of Juan de Torres and Leonor Zegarra.

44. APS (GL 797288), BMVC, Book II, fs 63v, 84, 112; (GL 797289), BMV, Book III, f 252; Larrain de Castro, "Zapallar," 61-62; Medina, Diccionario, 408, 859-860.

45. Mellafe, Esclavitud, 60-65, Introducción, passim; Rout, 41-43; Haring 329-333.

46. Flusche and Korth, Forgotten Females, 15, 22-23, analyze these cases further.

47. Roa y Ursúa, 207.

48. Ibid., 26-27, 381, 556.

49. Laval, Médicos, 46-48.

50. Actas, 77-82, 109 (1622: Oct. 8, 13, 14; 1623: Jan. 10); session of Oct. 12, 1622, in XXXVIII, 199-201; XXX, 106-108 (1629: Jan 25). See also Jara, "Asientos," 21-95; Flusche and Korth, Forgotten

Females, 30-31, 61-63; Meza Villalobos, 115-116.

51. See also Flusche and Korth, Forgotten Females, 62-63.

52. Genealogical data can be found in Thayer Ojeda, Santiago, 136-138, 178, 219; Roa y Ursúa, 44-45, 402; Espejo, Nobiliario, 277-282.

53. Partidas, Partida VI, title 15, law 5, allowed a father to give his son weapons and a horse necessary for becoming a knight; the value of such gifts was not divisible among the other heirs.

54. Thayer Ojeda, Santiago, 219, 227; Actas, XXVIII, 88, 95 (1622: Nov. 4, Dec. 9).

55. Actas, XXV, 518-522 (1621: Nov. 9).

56. APS (GL 797288), BMVC, Book II, fs 28v, 31, 41v; (GL 797289), BMV, Book IV, fs 14v, 30v, 75, 89, 101; Amunátegui Solar, Mayorazgos, I, 198-208; Thayer Ojeda, Santiago, 120, 165, 167-168, 192; Roa y Ursúa, 50-51, 207, 316-317, 427, 477. Espejo, Nobiliario, 178-180. When the notary Manuel died in 1670, there were thirteen living Toro y Cifuentes children.

57. Espejo, Nobiliario, 179-181, 876-879.

Epilogue

1. Góngora, "Social Stratification," 430-435, and Encomenderos, 103-112, 126-129, 138-172.

2. Góngora, Encomenderos, 146, 148, 168.

3. Carvallo Goyeneche, II, 474-475; Amunátegui Solar, Mayorazgos, I, 202-203, 210, 212-217; Espejo, Nobiliario, 194; Flusche, "Exports," 496; Actas, XLIII, 255-258 (1695: May 6); L, xliv-xlv, lxii.

4. APS (GL 797288), BMVC, Book II, f 63v; Medina, Diccionario, 408; Actas, XXXIV, 268-271 (1652: Oct. 30). Doña Antonia was the granddaughter of Inocencio Martínez de Aparicio and doña María de Escobar. The latter's godparents in 1621 were Alvaro Rodríguez and his wife doña Isabel Suárez, APS (GL 797289), BMV, Book III, f 252.

5. Amunátegui Solar, <u>Mayorazgos</u>, I, 201, 204-208, and "Institución del mayorazgo Toro Mazote," Santiago, Dec. 5, 1704, 223-230; Larraín de Castro, "Zapallar," 58-61.

6. Amunátegui Solar, <u>Mayorazgos</u>, I, 208-217; Larraín de Castro, "Zapallar," 61-68; Medina, <u>Diccionario</u>, 859-860; Roa y Ursúa, 340, 591; Thayer Ojeda, "Aguirre," 41. Doña Ignacia's parents were Gaspar Hidalgo y Aparicio Escobar and doña María de Zavala y Zapata. Marriages between relatives were not uncommon in colonial Spanish America. Certain degrees of consanguinity were impediments to marriage, but canonical dispensations could be obtained.

7. Amunátegui Solar, <u>Mayorazgos</u>, I, 208; Barbier, "Elite," 419-420, <u>Bourbon Chile</u>, 40-48. According to Barbier's eighteenth-century perspective, the creation of the Toro Mazote-Caldera entail placed the family in the old elite, but he is defining "old" and "new" elites with rather different criteria than those used here.

8. Larraín, "Papudo," 149-150.

9. Amunátegui Solar, <u>Mayorazgos</u>, I, 304-306, 316; Góngora, <u>Encomenderos</u>, 146, 148, 174, 185-186; <u>Actas</u>, XXX, 156-158 (1630: Feb. 23); Thayer Ojeda, <u>Familia</u>, 82-88, 97. Doña Antonia appointed a male deputy to serve as administrator of the pueblo.

10. <u>Actas</u>, XXV, 416-418, 435-441 (1620: Dec. 14, 1621: Jan. 15); Amunátegui Solar, <u>Mayorazgos</u>, I, 306-307; Thayer Ojeda, <u>Familia</u>, 79-82; Lohmann Villena, <u>Americanos</u>, II, 190; Silva Castro, 37-38.

11. <u>Actas</u>, XXV, 464-467 (1621: March 4).

12. APS (GL 797289), BMV, Book IV, fs 11v, 26, 50v, 53v; Amunátegui Solar, <u>Mayorazgos</u>, I, 307-312; Thayer Ojeda, <u>Familia</u>, 84, 88-90 and note 26; Espejo, <u>Nobiliario</u>, 41-43, 754, 874-876; don Francisco Fernando to doña Antonia de Aguilera y Estrada, Puerto Bello, June 20, 1637, in "Epistolario," 129-130. Don Fernando de Irarrázaval y Zárate had two illegitimate children.

13. "Epistolario," 125-134, cited above includes letters from don Francisco de Irarrázaval y Zárate, don Francisco Fernando, don José, and doña Francisca Antonia. Don José enjoyed the patronage of his paternal aunt doña Leonor de Recalde. The king granted the marqués de Valparaíso an income of 4,000 ducats from a vacant Peruvian encomienda by royal decree, Escorial, July 19, 1614, in Medina, Diccionario, 422-425.

14. Amunátegui Solar, Mayorazgos, I, 310-311; Espejo, Nobiliario, 526-531, 874-875; Góngora, Encomenderos, 149-150; Silva i Molina, 21-22; APS (GL 797288), BMVC, Book II, fs 108, 112. The compadres of doña Catalina Lorenza and don Juan Rodulfo included don Jorge de Ribera, the son of a former governor, and his maternal grandmother doña Inés de Córdoba, who was related to doña Antonia de Aguilera y Estrada.

15. Actas, XXXIII, 437-448 (1659: Dec. 6,9). Don Antonio Alfonso was a regidor when he became the corregidor; he was an alcalde in 1659, and in 1653 purchased a place as a councilman that he exercised for a short time. See ibid., 402-403 (1649: April 16); XXXIV, 377-381 (1653: Dec. 30; 1654: Jan. 1); XXXV, 442-443 (1659: Feb. 28).

16. Ibid., XXXIII, 317-324 (1648: Nov. 24).

17. Espejo, Nobiliario, 278, 624-625, 876; Thayer Ojeda, Santiago, 124, 228, 236-237, 244, Familia, 92-94; Amunátegui Solar, Mayorazgos, I, 311-312; Roa y Ursúa, 207-208, 422, 443-444, 460; Mujica, 28, 201. Doña Nicolasa's paternal grandfather Jerónimo Zapata de Mayorga became the treasurer of Santiago in 1612 and the alcalde of moradores in 1621, Actas, XXIV, 324 (1612: May 18); XXV, 430-431, 445-447 (1621: Jan. 9, 18). Her maternal grandfather Jerónimo de Benavides was also a treasury official in Santiago, the alcalde de vecinos in 1605, and the corregidor of Santiago in 1593 and 1606, ibid., XX, 438-446, 453-454 (1593: May 5, 6); Carvallo Goyeneche, II, 471-473.

18. Lohmann Villena, Americanos, II, 187;

Thayer Ojeda, Familia, 267.

19. Amunátegui Solar, Mayorazgos, I, 231-270, 313-322; Barbier, "Elite," 419, 421, Bourbon Chile, 44; Espejo, Nobiliario, 178-181, 624-625; Larraín, "Pullally," 118-119, "García de Cáceres," 31-113; Góngora, Encomenderos, 153; Thayer Ojeda, Familia, 97-120; APS (GL 797288), BMVC, Book II, fs 99v, 196v.

20. Eyzaguirre, 152, 200; APS (GL 797316), M, Book I, f 46v.

21. Amunátegui Solar, Mayorazgos, I, 268-270, 322-327; Mujica, 29; Espejo, Nobiliario, 180-181, 876-878; Thayer Ojeda, Familia, 121-127.

22. Larraín, "Pullally," 122-124, "Papudo," 148-149; Amunátegui Solar, Mayorazgos, I, 329-332, and "Institución del mayorazgo Irarrázaval," Santiago, Oct. 2, 1728, 355-363; Flusche and Korth, Forgotten Females, 27.

23. Espejo, Nobiliario, 177, 181, 194-195, 870, 879, provides illustrations and descriptions of the crests.

24. Ibid., 180-181, 567-568, 656-657, 878; Thayer Ojeda, Familia, 130-133.

25. José Perfecto de Salas, "Lista de algunos sujetos principales del reino de Chile, . . . desde Valparaíso a Santiago," in Amunátegui Solar, Personajes, 262.

BIBLIOGRAPHY

Primary Sources

Actas del cabildo de Santiago. 28 vols. In
 Historiadores and cited by the corresponding
 volume number of that Colección.
Andrews, Kenneth R., ed. The Last Voyage of Drake and
 Hawkins. Hakluyt Society, second series, no.
 142. Cambridge, 1972.
Archivo de la parroquia de el sagrario Santiago de
 Chile. Microfilms of cathedral parish records
 in the Genealogical Library. Salt Lake City.
Bermúdez Plata, Cristóbal, ed. Catálogo de pasajeros
 a Indias durante los siglos XVI, XVII y XVIII.
 3 vols. Consejo superior de investigaciones
 científicas. Seville, 1940-1946.
Bibar, Gerónimo. Crónica y relación copiosa y
 verdadera de los reynos de Chile. Facsimile
 edition with a transcription by Irving A.
 Leonard. 1966.
Caro de Torres, Francisco. Hechos de don Alonso de
 Sotomayor. Edited with an Introduction by
 Diego Barros Arana. In Historiadores, V.
_____. Historia de las órdenes militares de
 Santiago, Calatrava y Alcántara ... Quoted in
 BHC, I, 280-299, and in Silva Castro, 33-34.

----

*Unless otherwise indicated, the place of publication
of works in Spanish is Santiago, Chile.

Carvallo Goyeneche, Vicente. *Descripción histórico-jeográfica del reino de Chile*. 3 vols. In *Historiadores*, VIII-X.

Chile. Archivo Nacional. Archivo de los Escribanos de Santiago.

Colección de documentos inéditos para la historia de Chile. First series. Edited by José Toribio Medina. 30 vols. 1888-1902.

Colección de documentos inéditos para la historia de Chile. Second series. Collected by José Toribio Medina. 6 vols. 1956-1963.

Colección de documentos inéditos para la historia de Hispano-América. 14 vols. Madrid, 1927-1932. (Some titles are...*Ibero-América*.)

Colección de documentos inéditos relativos al descubrimiento, conquista y colonización de las posesiones españolas en América y Oceanía. 42 vols. Madrid, 1864-1884.

Colección de historiadores de Chile y documentos relativos a la historia nacional. Edited by José Toribio Medina et al. 51 vols. 1861-1953.

Cortés, Hernando. *Five Letters of Cortés to the Emperor*. Translated by J. Bayard Morris. New York, 1962.

Díaz del Castillo, Bernal. *The Discovery and Conquest of Mexico, 1517-1521*. Translated by A.O. Maudslay. New York, 1956.

"Epistolario de la familia Yrarrázaval en el siglo XVII." *BACH*, no. 41 (1949), 125-134.

Ercilla y Zúniga, Alonso de. La Araucana. Edited
  with notes and appendices by José Toribio
  Medina. 5 vols. 1910-1918.
El fuero real de España. In Martínez Alcubilla,
  Códigos.
Góngora, Mario, ed. "Documentos inéditos sobre la
  encomienda en Chile," part 2. RCHG, no. 124
  (1956), 113-176.
Góngora Marmolejo, Alonso de. Historia de Chile desde
  su descubrimiento hasta el año de 1575. Edited
  by Francisco Esteve Barba. In Biblioteca de
  autores españoles, CXXXI, Madrid, 1960.
Irarrázaval, don Francisco de. Letter to the Council
  of the Indies. Lima, Nov. 10, 1563. In DIF,
  XXIX, 292-293.
⎯⎯⎯. Letter to the king. Lima, Nov. 20, 1564. In
  DIF, XXIX, 382-384.
⎯⎯⎯. Letter to the king. Lima, Feb. 1, 1566. In
  DIS, I, 57-59.
Jara, Alvaro, ed. "Fuentes para la historia del
  trabajo en el reino de Chile," part 4. BACH,
  no. 61 (1959), 156-181.
Konetzke, Richard, ed. Colección de documentos para
  la historia de la formación social de
  Hispanoamérica,1493-1810. 3 vols in 5.
  Consejo superior de investigaciones científicas.
  Madrid, 1953-1962.
Leyes de Toro. In Martínez Alcubilla, Códigos.
Lillo, Ginés de. Mensuras de Ginés de Lillo. 2 vols.
  In Historiadores, XLVIII-XLIX.

Lockhart, James and Enrique Otte, eds. and trans.
   Letters and People of the Spanish Indies: The
   Sixteenth Century. Cambridge Latin American
   Studies, no. 22. New York, 1976.
Mariño de Lobera, Pedro. Crónica del reino de Chile.
   Edited by Francisco Esteve Barba. In Biblioteca
   de autores españoles, CXXXI, Madrid, 1960.
Martínez Alcubilla, Marcelo, comp. Códigos antiguos
   de España. 2 vols. Madrid, 1885.
Medina, José Toribio, ed. Biblioteca hispano-chilena,
   3 vols. 1897-1899.
"Los oficiales reales y el fiscal de S. M. en el
   pleito contra Juan Gómez y otros sobre la
   posesión de los repartimientos de indios del
   valle de Quillota y Mapochoes," 1561. In DIF,
   XI, 311-419.
Ovalle, Alonso de. Histórica del reyno de Chile.
   Escritores de Chile, no. 1. 1969.
Parry, John H. and Robert G. Keith, eds. New Iberian
   World: A Documentary History of the Discovery
   and Settlement of Latin America to the Early
   17th Century. 5 vols. New York, 1984.
"Probanza del capitán Juan Gómez é otros autos del
   pleito seguido á su instancia contra don
   Francisco de Irarrázaval y el fiscal de S.M.
   sobre la posesión del repartimiento de indios
   del valle de Quillota y Mapochoes en las
   provincias de Chile," 1561. In DIF, XI, 419-
   556.

"Probanza de don Francisco Irarrázaval en la causa seguida á su instancia contra Juan Gómez y el fiscal de Su Majestad, sobre la tenencia de ciertos indios del valle de Quillota en las provincias de Chile," 1565. In DIF, XXIII, 53-93.

"Probanza...del gobernador Pedro de Villagrán." In DIF, XXIX, 433-531.

"Probanza de los méritos y servicios de don Francisco de Irarrázaval," 1559. In DIF, XXIII, 39-53.

"Probanzas de Juan Gómez Almagro y Antonio Tarabajano en el pleito seguido entre ámbos sobre la encomienda de indios de Topocalma," 1556-1561. In DIF, XI, 5-311.

Recopilación de leyes de los reynos de las Indias. 3 vols. Madrid, 1943.

Rosales, Diego de. Historia general del reino de Chile. Edited by Benjamín Vicuña Mackenna. 3 vols. Valparaíso, 1877-1878.

Royal cédula to the governor of Chile, Toledo, Jan. 22, 1561. In DIS, I, 18-19.

Salas, José Perfecto de. "Lista de algunos sujetos principales del reino de Chile, . . . desde Valparaíso a Santiago." In Amunátegui Solar, Personajes, 234-272.

Servicios de capitán Pedro de Olmos de Aguilera, 1574, 1582. In DIF, XXV, 29-36, 180-219.

Las Siete Partidas. Translated by Samuel Parsons Scott. Chicago, 1931.

Solórzano y Pereyra, Juan de. Política indiana. Annotated by Francisco Ramiro de Valenzuela. 5 vols. Buenos Aires, 1930.

"Testimonio de ciertos pliegos y documentos entregados á la real audiencia de Chile," Aug. 12, 1567. In DIS, I, 97-100.

Testimony and sentence in the residencia of Governor García Hurtado de Mendoza. In DIF, XXVIII, 377-433.

"Título de encomienda de indios dado por Pedro de Villagra á don Francisco de Irarrázaval y real cédula y poder sobre el mismo título." In DIS, I, 17-24.

Valdivia, Pedro de. Cartas de Pedro de Valdivia, que tratan del descubrimiento y conquista de Chile. Edited by Francisco Esteve Barba. In Biblioteca de autores españoles, CXXXI, Madrid, 1960.

The Visigothic Code (Forum Judicum). Translated by Samuel Parsons Scott. Boston, 1910.

Vivar, Gerónimo de. Gerónimo de Vivar: Crónica y relación copiosa y verdadera de los reinos de Chile (1558). Edited by Leopoldo Saez-Godoy. Bibliotheca Ibero-Americana, no. 27. Berlin, 1979.

BIBLIOGRAPHY

Secondary Sources

Amunátegui, Miguel Luis. <u>Los precursores de la independencia de Chile</u>. 3 vols. 1870-1872.

Amunátegui Solar, Domingo. <u>Las encomiendas de indíjenas en Chile</u>. 2 vols. 1909-1910.

_____. <u>Personajes de la colonia</u>. 1925.

_____. <u>La sociedad chilena del siglo XVIII: mayorazgos i títulos de Castilla</u>. 3 vols. 1901-1904.

Andrews, Kenneth R. <u>Drake's Voyages: A Re-Assessment of Their Place in Elizabethan Maritime Expansion</u>. London, 1967.

_____. <u>Elizabethan Privateering: English Privateering during the Spanish War, 1585-1603</u>. Cambridge, 1964.

Barbier, Jacques A. "Elite and Cadres in Bourbon Chile." <u>HAHR</u>, 52 (Aug., 1972), 416-435.

_____. <u>Reform and Politics in Bourbon Chile, 1755-1796</u>. Ottawa, 1980.

Burkholder, Mark A. and D.S. Chandler. <u>From Impotence to Authority: The Spanish Crown and the American Audiencias, 1687-1808</u>. Columbia, 1977.

Cano Roldán, Sor Imelda. <u>La mujer en el reyno de Chile</u>. 1980.

Castro, Américo. <u>The Structure of Spanish History</u>. Princeton, 1954.

Cavazos Garza, Israel. <u>Cedulario autobiográfico de pobladores y conquistadores de Nuevo León</u>. Monterrey, México, 1964.

Concha, Manuel. *Crónica de la Serena desde su fundación hasta nuestros días, 1549-1870*. Serena, 1871.

Edwards, Agustín. *Peoples of Old*. London, 1929.

Errázuriz, Crescente. *Historia de Chile sin gobernador, 1554-1557*. 1912.

Espejo, Juan Luis. *Nobiliario de la capitanía general de Chile*. 2nd ed. 1966.

_____, ed. *La provincia de Cuyo del reino de Chile*. 2 vols. 1954.

Eyzaguirre, Jaime. *Historia de Chile: génesis de la nacionalidad*. 2nd ed. 1964.

Flusche, Della M. "The Cabildo and Public Health in Seventeenth-Century Santiago, Chile." *TAm*, 29 (Oct., 1972), 173-190.

_____. "Chilean Councilmen and Export Policies, 1600-1699." *TAm*, 36 (April, 1980), 478-498.

_____. "City Councilmen and the Church in Seventeenth-Century Chile." *Records of the American Catholic Historical Society of Philadelphia*, 81 (Sept., 1970), 176-190.

Flusche, Della M. and Eugene H. Korth. *Forgotten Females: Women of African and Indian Descent in Colonial Chile, 1535-1800*. Detroit, 1983.

_____. "A Dowry Office in Seventeenth-Century Chile." *The Historian: A Journal of History*, 49 (Feb., 1987), 204-222.

Gibson, Charles. *Spain in America*. The New American Nation Series. New York, 1966.

Góngora, Mario. Encomenderos y estancieros: estudios acerca de la constitución social aristocrática de Chile después de la conquista, 1580-1660. 1970.

_____. "Los 'hombres ricos' de Santiago y de la Serena a través de las cuentas del quinto real, 1567-1577." RCHG, no. 131 (1963), 23-46.

_____. "Urban Social Stratification in Colonial Chile." HAHR, 55 (Aug., 1975), 421-448.

Hanke, Lewis. The Spanish Struggle for Justice in the Conquest of America. 2nd ed. Boston, 1965.

Haring, C.H. The Spanish Empire in America. New York, 1947.

Jara, Alvaro. "Los asientos de trabajo y la provisión de mano de obra para los noencomenderos en la ciudad de Santiago, 1586-1600." RCHG, no. 125 (1957), 21-95.

_____. El salario de los indios y los sesmos del oro en la tasa de Santillán. 1960.

Kamen, Henry. The Spanish Inquisition. New York, 1965.

Korth, Eugene H., S. J. Spanish Policy in Colonial Chile: The Struggle for Social Justice, 1535-1700. Stanford, 1968.

Korth, Eugene H., S. J. and Della M. Flusche. "Dowry and Inheritance in Colonial Spanish America: Peninsular Law and Chilean Practice." TAm, 43 (April, 1987), 395-410.

Lafuente Machain, R. de. Los conquistadores del Río de la Plata. 2nd. ed. Buenos Aires, 1943.

Larraín, Carlos J. " 'Lo Arcaya' y tierras de Colina." BACH, no. 61 (1959), 52-90.

_____. "Diego García de Cáceres, el conquistador." BACH, no. 65 (1961), 31-113.

_____. "La encomienda de Pullally." BACH, no. 47 (1952), 97-135.

_____. "Francisco de Riberos, conquistador de Chile." BACH, no. 16 (1941), 105-140.

_____. "Papudo, breve relato cronológico." BACH, no. 68 (1963), 137-180.

Larraín de Castro, Carlos J. "Los orígenes de Zapallar." BACH, no. 12 (1940), 37-84.

Laval M., Enrique. Historia del hospital San Juan de Dios de Santiago. 1949.

_____. Noticias sobre los médicos en Chile en los siglos XVI, XVII y XVIII. 1958.

Lockhart, James. The Men of Cajamarca: A Social and Biographical Study of the First Conquerors of Peru. University of Texas Institute of Latin American Studies, Latin American Monographs, no. 27. Austin, 1972.

_____. Spanish Peru, 1532-1560: A Colonial Society. Madison, 1968.

Lohmann Villena, Guillermo. Los americanos en las órdenes nobiliarias, 1529-1900. 2 vols. Consejo superior de investigaciones científicas. Madrid, 1947.

_____. Los ministros de la audiencia de Lima, 1700-1821. Escuela de estudios hispano-americanos de Sevilla, no. 222. Seville, 1974.

Loveman, Brian. Chile: The Legacy of Hispanic
   Capitalism. New York, 1979.
Medina, José Toribio. Diccionario biográfico colonial
   de Chile. 1906.
_____. Historia del tribunal del Santo Oficio de la
   Inquisición en Chile. 2 vols. 1890.
Mellafe, Rolando. El esclavitud en hispano-américa.
   Buenos Aires, 1964.
_____. La introducción de la esclavitud negra en
   Chile: tráfico y rutas. 1959.
Mendiburu, Manuel de. Diccionario histórico-
   biográfico del Perú. 2nd ed. 15 vols. Lima,
   1931-1938.
Meza Villalobos, Nestor. La conciencia política
   chilena durante la monarquía. 1958.
Mörner, Magnus. "Economic Factors and Stratification
   in Colonial Spanish America with Special Regard
   to Elites." HAHR, 63 (May, 1983), 335-369.
_____. Race Mixture in the History of Latin America.
   Boston, 1967.
Mujica, J. Nobleza colonial de Chile. 1927.
Mujica de la Fuente, J. "La familia del adelantado don
   Diego de Almagro." BACH, no. 7 (1936), 295-321.
Ots Capdequí, José María. Historia del derecho
   español en América y del derecho indiano.
   Madrid, 1969.
Painter, Sidney. French Chivalry: Chivalric Ideas
   and Practices in Mediaeval France. Ithaca,
   1957.

Parry, J. H. The Sale of Public Office in the Spanish Indies under the Hapsburgs. Ibero-Americana, no. 37, Berkeley, 1953.

Ramón Folch, José Armando. "La sociedad española de Santiago de Chile entre 1581 y 1596 (estudio de grupos)." Historia, no. 4 (1965), 191-228.

Roa y Ursúa, Luis de. El reyno de Chile, 1535-1810, estudio histórico, genealógico y biográfico. Valladolid, 1945.

Rout, Leslie B., Jr. The African Experience in Spanish America: 1502 to the Present Day. Cambridge Latin American Studies, no. 23. Cambridge, 1976.

Schäfer, Ernesto. El consejo real y supremo de las Indias. 2 vols. Escuela de estudios hispano-americanos de Sevilla. Seville, 1935-1947.

Silva Castro, Raúl. Los Irarrázaval de Chile según cronistas e historiadores, 1557-1957. Buenos Aires, 1957.

Silva i Molina, Abraham de. Oidores de la real audiencia de Santiago durante el siglo XVII. 1903.

Thayer Ojeda, Tomás. La familia Irarrázaval en Chile. 1931.

_____. Formación de la sociedad chilena y censo de la población de Chile en los años de 1540 a 1565. 3 vols. 1939-1941.

_____. "Francisco de Aguirre." RCHG, no. 64 (1929), 5-43.

_____. <u>Santiago durante el siglo XVI: constitución de la propiedad urbana i noticias biográficas de sus primeros pobladores</u>. 1905.

Thayer Ojeda, Tomás and Carlos J. Larraín. <u>Valdivia y sus compañeros</u>. 1950.

Vargas Ugarte, Rubén, S. J. <u>Historia general del Perú</u>. Edited by Carlos Milla Batres. 10 vols. Lima, 1966-1971.

INDEX

Aguilera y Estrada, doña Antonia de, 48, 63, 85-86, 161, 163, 164, 165, 166, 175, 189.
Aguirre, doña María Martínez de, 10.
Agurto, Gaspar de, 187-188.
Agurto, don Jerónimo de, 176.
Ahumada Gavilán, Juan de, 143.
Alderete, Jerónimo de, 10, 11, 13, 61.
Almagro, Diego de, 39.
Altamirano, Diego García, 47, 48.
Alvarado, García de, 45.
Andía Irarrázaval, doña Francisca Antonia de, 166.
Angolans, 149-151.
Aparicio y Escobar, doña María de, 160.
Araucanians, 5, 11, 14-15, 17, 18, 19, 20, 123, 124-125, 126, 131, 136-137.
Astorga, Juan de, 156, 176.
Audiencia, of Concepción, 58-59, 90, 103, 111; of Lima, 15, 17, 27, 36, 37, 43, 58, 91, 128; of Santiago, 106, 109, 111, 112, 113, 115, 127, 128, 129, 130, 131, 134, 138, 152-153.
Avendaño y Villela, doña Sebastiana de, 128.

Azoca, doña Ana María de, 115.
Azoca, Antonio de, 138, 166, 175.
Azoca, doña Isabel de, 138.
Barambio, Antonio de, 160.
Barbier, Jacques A., xii, xiv.
Barona, Andrés, 181.
Bello, Alonso, 149, 193.
Beltrán de Magaña, Juan 43, 44, 45, 47, 48, 51, 53.
Benavides, doña Jerónima, 168.
Biafrans, 149, 151.
Bocanegra, Antonio de, 155, 180-193 passim.
Bravo de Naveda, don Fernando, 103-104, 107, 132, 149, 150, 190.
Bravo de Saravia, don Francisco, 169, 170.
Bravo de Saravia, don Jerónimo, 156, 168, 169.
Bravo de Saravia, doña Marcela Norberta, 170.
Bravo de Saravia, doctor Melchor, 59, 61, 62, 74.
Bravo de Saravia, don Ramiriáñez, 74, 174, 175.
Bravo de Saravia Andía Irarrázaval, don Miguel, 163, 170, 171.

Bravo de Saravia (y Henestrosa), doña Agustina, 169, 176.
Bravo de Saravia (y Henestrosa), doña Catalina, 170.
Bravo de Saravia (y Henestrosa), don Jerónimo, 170.
Briceño, Agustín, 42, 43, 176.

Cáceres, doña Juana de, 143.
Cajal, don Juan, 149.
Caldera, Juan Antonio, 160, 161.
Caldera, Juan Luis, 160.
Campofrío de Carvajal, Alonso, 73, 174.
Campo Lantadilla, Alonso del, 144-145, 146, 147, 149, 150.
Campo Lantadilla, doña Magdalena del, 148, 160.
Cárcamo Valdés, Diego, 115.
Caro de Torres, Francisco, 84-85.
Carvajal y Ulloa, don Fernando, 113.
Casas, Juan Bautista de, 141, 148.
Castañeda, don Gregorio de, 180.
Celada, don Alonso de, 112, 130.
Celada, doctor Gabriel de, 111.
Celada, doña Luisa de, 112-113.
Celada, doña María de, 113.
Cerda y Sotomayor, doctor Cristóbal de la, 127-131, 132, 164-165.
Charles V, 1, 10, 16.

Cid Maldonado, Alonso, 130.
Cid Maldonado, doña María, 144.
Cifontes, doña Ana Félix, 153.
Cifontes, Gabriel, 149.
Cifuentes, doña Francisca de, 121.
Cifuentes Hidalgo, doña Juana de, 121, 141, 153, 156-157, 160, 162, 176.
Coba y Lucero, doña Francisca de la, 129, 151.
Concepción, 16, 17, 118.
Córdoba, Alonso de, 153-154.
Córdoba y Morales, Ambrosio de, 153-154
Córdoba y Morales, doña Inés de, 107-108, 154.
Costilla, Jerónimo, 58.
Council of the Indies, 22, 23, 25, 35, 66.
Cuevas, Juan de, 68.
Cuevas Villaroel, don Sancho de las, 143.
Cuyo, 132, 133, 134, 139.

Díaz Hidalgo, Gaspar, 181, 183, 185, 188-192 passim.
Díaz Hidalgo, Simón, 121.
Díaz Vera, Antonio, 47, 48, 53.
Drake, Sir Francis, 83.

Edwards, Agustín, 2.
Elguea, Pedro de, 191.
Elvira, doña (cacica of Talagante), 167.
Encomiendas, 2-4, 19, 22-24, 26-33, 35-56 passim, 59, 67-71 passim, 75, 77-78, 82-83, 85, 87-88, 101, 110-113, 115-116, 119, 123, 125, 138-139, 144-145, 161, 163-165, 167, 170, 184.

Eraso, don Domingo, 110.
Eraso, don Francisco de, 110, 130, 152, 184.
Eraso y Ubitarte, doña Beatriz de, 110.
Ercilla y Zúñiga, don Alonso de, 9, 10, 11, 16, 18, 56, 73.
Escobar y López, Alonso de, 144, 145, 147.
Escobar y Torres, doña Beatriz de, 144-146.
Escobar y Torres, doña Clementa de, 144-147.
Escobar y Torres, doña María de, 146, 147, 148.
Escobedo, doña Francisca de, 42, 47, 48, 189.
Escobedo, Juan de, 42, 43, 90.
Espinosa, doña María de, 38.
Espinosa Caracol, Francisco de, 187-188.
Estrada, doña Antonia de, 62.

Fernández de Aguiar, Jorge, 194.
Fernández de Montoya, Juan, 143.
Ferreira y Aponte, Gonzalo, 141-142, 149, 150, 156.
Flamenco, Juan, 149-150.
Flores, Bartolomé, 167.
Fuenmayor, Bernardino, 183.

Gallegos, Bernabé, 140.
García de Castro, Lope, 58.
García Melo, Juan, 186-187.
García de Navia, Alvar, 62, 86.
García Ramón, Alonso, 62 105, 118.
García de Valles, Juan, 181.
Gavilán, doña Juana, 143.

Girón y Montenegro, don Florián, 179-180, 183.
Gómez, Juan, 32, 36, 37, 38, 39-44, 46-56, 135, 189.
Gómez de Miranda, Duarte, 188-189.
Gómez de las Montanas, Francisco, 69-70.
Góngora, Mario, xi-xii, 159.
Góngora Marmolejo, Alonso de, 65.
González de Andía Irarrázaval, Antón, 9-10.
Gónzalez de la Cruz, Martín, 109.
González Marmolejo, don Rodrigo, 27, 36, 37.
González Montero, don Diego, 138-139, 165, 179-180.
González de San Nicolás, Gil, 15, 36.
Granada, Juan Alonso, 191.
Guajardo, doña Isabel, 166, 175.
Guzmán, doña Aldonza de, 150.

Hanke, Lewis, 7, 15.
Henestrosa, doña Marcela de, 169-170.
Henríquez, don Juan, 176.
Hermua, San Juan de, 151, 191.
Hernández, Andrés, 95-97.
Hernández, Cristóbal, 100.
Hernández Girón, Francisco, 11.
Hernández de la Serna, Andrés, 97.
Hernández de la Serna, Gaspar, 141, 153.

Hernández de la Serna, doña Luisa, 156.
Hernández de la Serna, Melchor, 97, 101, 118.
Hidalgo, doña Ignacia, 162, 163, 171.
Hidalgo y Aparicio Escobar, doña Antonia, 160.
Hurtado de Mendoza, don Andrés, 13, 21.
Hurtado de Mendoza, don García, 3, 13, 14-16, 17, 18, 20, 21, 23, 25, 36-37, 41, 42, 52, 73, 76, 82.
Hurtado de Mendoza, Jerónimo, 125.

Ibañez y Barroeta, Andrés de, 69.
Indians, 14, 15, 20, 21, 39, 71, 78-79, 83, 123-126, 131; female, 72, 77, 98, 139; occupations of, 78, 131-133, 151-153, 185, 187-188.
Inquisition, Holy Office of the, 67.
Irarrázaval (y Aguilera), doña Catalina Lorenza de, 166-168 passim.
Irarrázaval y Andía, don Antonio de, 159.
Irarrázaval y Andía, don Antonio Alfonso de, 166-169, 171, 175.
Irarrázaval y Andía, don Francisco de, 8-13, 16-33, 36-38, 40, 41, 43-49, 51-59, 63-72 passim, 84, 164, 170, 174.
Irarrázaval y Andía, don Francisco Fernando de, 166.
Irarrázaval y Andía, don José de, 166, 175.
Irarrázaval y Andía, don Menjón de, 10.
Irarrázaval y Bravo de Saravia, don Antonio de, 169-170.
Irarrázaval y Bravo de Saravia, don Juan de, 175-176.
Irarrázaval y Zapata, don Fernando Francisco de, 169, 175.
Irarrázaval (y Zárate), don Carlos de, 80.
Irarrázaval (y Zárate), don Fernando de, 63, 80, 82-83, 85-86, 163-166, 175.
Irarrázaval (y Zárate), don Francisco de, 72-73, 166.

Jaramillo, Bernardo, 193.
Jiménez, Juana, 40.
Jiménez de Lorca, Andrés de, 139, 184.
Jorge de Segura, Gaspar, 80.
Juana, Princess, 11, 12.
Justiniano, doña Catalina, 150, 190-191.

Korth, Eugene H., S.J., xiii.

Lazo de la Vega, Francisco, 104, 106, 107, 113, 115.
León, Juan Andrés de, 143, 149, 193.
Lisperguer, don Juan Rodulfo, 166-167, 168.
Lisperguer, Pedro, 167.
Lisperguer, don Pedro, 132, 152.
Lisperguer y Flores, doña Catalina, 156.

Lisperguer y Irarrázaval, doña Catalina, 169.
Llanos, Diego de, 18.
Loaisa, doña María Clara, de, 180.
Lockhart, James, xiv.
López, Rodrigo, 140.
López de Azoca, Luis, 66, 69, 70.
López de Córdoba, Juan, 153.
Loveman, Brian, xii-xiii.
Lugo, Francisco de, 69.

Machado, Fernando, 128, 153.
Machado, doctor Pedro, 138, 179.
Maldonado, Bartolomé, 113.
Maldonado de Silva, Francisco, 151.
Marín y Riberos, doña Josefa de, 161, 162.
Mariño de Lobera, Pedro, 18.
Martínez, Francisco, 98.
Martínez de Aparicio, Inocencio, 146-148 passim, 183, 187.
Mazo de Alderete, Diego de, 37, 38, 48.
Medina, Juan Luis de, 143.
Meneses, doña Constanza de, 61.
Meneses, Francisco de, 170.
Meza Villalobos, Néstor, 4-5.
Millapidum, don Francisco 68-70.
Miranda, Francisco de, 184.
Miranda, doña Magdalena de, 100.
Molina, Jerónimo de, 78, 79, 90, 192-193.

Molina y Paraguez, Luis de, 192-193.
Montesa, doña María, 38.
Morales y Córdoba, Diego de, 154, 182.
Morales Negrete, Juan de, 80, 130.
Mörner, Magnus, xi, xii, 2.
Narijado, Domingo del, 151.
Narváez y Valdelomar, Gaspar de, 153, 185, 186.
Navarro, doña Beatriz, 156, 176.
New Laws of 1542, 36.
Niño de Estrada, doña Catalina, 62-63, 85.
Nunneries, 73, 143-147 passim.

Olavarría, Tomás de, 104, 110, 178.
Olmos de Aguilera, Pedro, the elder, 86.
Olmos de Aguilera, Pedro, the younger, 62, 86.
Oñez de Loyola, don Martín García, 82.
Orense, Gaspar, 39-40, 42.
Orozco, doña Ursula de, 42.
Ortiz de Gaete, doña Marina, 10, 61, 73, 183.
Osores de Ulloa, don Pedro de, 130, 131, 138, 139, 194.
Osorio de Cáceres, doña Isabel, 74, 97, 174, 175.
Ovalle, doña Agustina de, 169.
Ovalle, don Francisco Rodríguez de, 139, 165, 169, 175.

Pacoa, encomienda and village of, 56, 67-71, 77-78, 83, 163.
Páez de la Serna, Francisco, 62.
Painter, Sidney, 5.
Pajuelo, doña Francisca, 192-193.
Pardo Maldonado, Arias, 44, 46, 49, 53.
Pardo Parraguez, doña Isabel, 193.
Pastene, Francisco, 190.
Pastene y Lantadilla, doña María, 165, 169, 175.
Pérez de Urasandi, Juan, 113, 114.
Philip II, 9, 10, 11, 12, 16, 17, 18, 22, 24, 25, 29, 30, 31, 32, 53, 54-56, 58, 75.
Philip III, 73, 105, 124, 125, 126.
Philip IV, 77, 124, 126, 127, 131.
Pizarro, don Cristóbal, 151, 191.
Portales y Meneses, doña Francisca, 170.
Portillo, Pedro del, 137, 188-189, 193.
Public office, proprietary, 93, 99-100, 104-107, 108-110, 117-119, 121-122, 133-134, 141-142, 159-160, 171, 177-178.

Quillota, encomienda of, 27-29, 32, 36-38, 43-45, 47, 49, 54-56, 57, 59.
Quiroga, Rodrigo de, 32, 58, 60, 65.

Ramón, doña Elena, 146.
Ramos, Juan, 139.

Rapel, encomienda and village of, 39-44, 46-47, 56, 67, 83, 85, 163-164.
Recalde, doña Leonor de (Irarrázaval y Zárate), 73.
Recalde, doña María de, 24, 29.
Ribera, Alonso de, 77, 100, 113, 114, 137, 194.
Riberos, doña Mariana de, 73, 174.
Riberos y Figueroa y Aguirre, don José de, 113.
Ricardo de Montalbán, doña Francisca, 111, 112.
Ríos, don Gonzalo de los, 152, 156.
Rivadeneira, don Juan de, 56, 189.
Rodríguez, Alvaro, 145, 146, 147, 148.
Rodríguez, Luis, 132.
Rojas y Puebla, Bartolomé de, 149, 150, 192, 193.
Rueda, doña Esperanza de, 10, 61.

Sáez de Galiano, Antolin, 136.
Salinas, Alonso de, 108, 153, 154, 182, 185.
Salinas y Córdoba, don Pedro de, 108, 113, 178.
Sánchez, Francisca, 181.
Sánchez, doña Tomasa, 181.
Santiago, cabildo of, 39, 65-67, 70, 90-92, 97, 99-100, 104-110, 114-115, 117-122, 124-127, 129-135, 140, 153, 154, 155, 164, 167; city of, 14, 24, 57, 59-60, 122-126 passim, 131-155 passim, 164-165.

Santiago, Juan de, 140.
Santillán, Hernando de, 15, 36.
Seco, Pedro, 140-141.
Serna, doña Elena de la, 97-103, 112, 117-118, 120, 135, 149-150, 176.
Serna, Magdalena de la, 95, 97, 98.
Silva Vargas, Juan de, 139.
Slaves, Indian, 88, 112, 119, 125; Negroid, 72, 112, 119, 134, 135, 146, 148-151, 188-192.
Soto, don Gaspar de, 106, 151.
Sotomayor, don Alonso de, 71-72, 74-85 passim, 99, 174-175.
Sotomayor, doña Jerónima de, 59, 61-62.
Sotomayor y Zárate, don Alonso de, 174-175.
Sotomayor y Zárate, don Carlos de, 84.
Sotomayor y Zárate, doña Lorenza de, 77, 166.
Suárez, doña Inés, 60.
Suárez, doña Isabel, 148.
Suárez de Figueroa, Garci, 68.
Suárez Fortuño, doña Nicolasa, 113.

Tapia, Sebastián de, 142.
Tarabajano, Antonio, 41-43, 56.
Tarabajano, Francisca de, 42-43, 176.
Tasa de Esquilache, 125, 127, 130, 131, 152, 165.
Thayer Ojeda, Tomás, 98-99.
Toledo, Viceroy Francisco de, 64, 65.
Toledo y Arbildo, Francisco de, 141-142.
Toro y Celada, doña Ana María de, 113.
Toro y Celada, doña Antonia de, 113.
Toro y Celada, doña Francisca de, 108, 113.
Toro y Celada, doña Gabriela de, 113.
Toro y Celada, don Pedro de, 112.
Toro y Cifuentes, Andrés de, 160-162.
Toro y Cifuentes, Francisco de, 156.
Toro y Cifuentes, Gabriel de, 156.
Toro y Cifuentes, doña Luisa de, 156, 160-162.
Toro y Cifuentes, Simón de, 156.
Toro y Córdoba, doña Apolinarda de, 110-111.
Toro y Córdoba, don Matías de, 108-110, 178.
Toro y Eraso, doña Francisca de, 109.
Toro y Eraso, Ginés de, 109, 178.
Toro Hidalgo, don Andrés de, 160-162, 171.
Toro Mazote, Ginés de (the elder), 80, 81, 98-105, 112, 117, 176, 178.
Toro Mazote (y la Serna), Andrés de, 103, 112-115, 120, 129, 131, 141, 145, 152, 154, 160, 182.
Toro Mazote (y la Serna), Ginés de (the younger), 103, 105-108, 111, 113, 117, 120, 121, 132, 140, 141, 154, 160, 178, 182, 183.

Toro Mazote (y la Serna), doña Juana de, 103, 104, 150, 176.
Toro Mazote (y la Serna), Luis de, 141, 154, 182, 193.
Toro Mazote (y la Serna), Manuel de, 103, 113, 117-122, 135-160 passim, 161, 162, 164, 165, 167, 171, 176, 178, 179ff.
Toro Mazote (y la Serna), doña María Magdalena de, 103, 104.
Torre, Pedro de la, 166.
Torres, doña Luisa de, 145.
Torres de Vera, Juan de, 59, 72, 75-76.

Ulloa, Francisco de, 19.
Ulloa y Lemos, Lope de, 127, 128, 129, 151.
Ureta, Juan Bautista de, 129, 151.

Valdivia, fort of, 120.
Valdivia, Pedro de, 1, 2, 10, 11, 14, 16, 39, 40, 42, 48, 50-51, 60, 61, 73, 86.
Valenzuela, don Juan de, 144.
Valiente de la Barra, Pedro, 194.
Varas, Juan, 174.
Villagra, Francisco de, 25, 37, 38, 40-41, 49.
Villagra, doña Mariana de, 189.
Villagra, Pedro de, 25, 26-28, 29, 32, 36, 37, 44, 45, 51, 54, 58.
Villarroel, Bishop Gaspar de, 120.
Vivero, Alvaro de, 186-187.

Yupanqui, doña Leonor, 64.

Zamudio, Andrés de, 141.
Zapata, Alonso de, 99.
Zapata de Mayorga, Francisco, 168.
Zapata de Mayorga, doña Nicolasa, 168-169.
Zárate, doña Angela de, 73.
Zárate, don Diego de, 73, 174.
Zárate, don Diego Ortiz de, 24.
Zárate, don Fernando de, 25, 26, 64, 72.
Zárate, doña Isabel de, 74-75, 77-78, 81, 83, 84, 85, 174, 175.
Zárate, don Juan Ortiz de, 26, 64-65.
Zárate, doña Juana de, 64-65, 72, 75-76.
Zárate, doña Lorenza de, 8, 24, 25, 26-27, 29, 45, 47-48, 55, 59-62, 63-64, 67, 71, 72, 73-74, 77-85, 120, 174.
Zúñiga, don Francisco de, 106.

Latin American Studies

1. David Craven, **The New Concept of Art and Popular Culture in Nicaragua Since the Revolution in 1979**
2. Della M. Flusche, **Two Families in Colonial Chile**